Modern Benford's Law

Benford's Law offers a powerful, data-driven approach to anomaly detection. Discovered 150 years ago, it wasn't until the 1990s that auditors began harnessing its potential for identifying irregularities in financial data. Today, the Benford's Law community spans a wide range of professions and academic disciplines.

This book provides the latest research-based techniques packaged for ready usage by auditors and audit analytics professionals. Discover how to use Benford's Law in continuous monitoring and pinpoint non-compliant vendors, accounts, or other groups. Visual examples demonstrate how to identify and interpret the most common patterns Benford's Law surfaces.

Auditors and assurance professionals will benefit from clear, practical explanations of advanced methods, making it easier to integrate these techniques into their workflows. Meanwhile, analytics and quantitative experts will find a rich toolkit of new techniques to enhance their capabilities. Whether you're new to Benford's Law or looking to deepen your expertise, this book equips you with the tools to transform how you detect anomalies in data.

Daniel J. McCarville is a recognized audit analytics professional, researcher, and speaker with more than a decade of experience developing advanced tools for auditors and compliance teams. He currently leads the audit analytics team at an S&P 500 insurance firm. His statistical expertise spans Benford's Law, machine learning, and simulation, which he applies to detect anomalies and strengthen decision-making.

His peer-reviewed research has introduced novel applications of Benford's Law and new methods for identifying irregularities in standardized test data. He has published in Emerald Open Research and received the National Legislative Program Evaluation Society's Impact Award multiple times.

Daniel has presented at major professional conferences, including IIA events, and frequently speaks at universities to inspire the next generation of data professionals. He holds a master's degree in political science from the University of Kansas, as well as Data Science from Eastern University. He also holds CIA and CRMA designations from the Institute of Internal Auditors and DASM certification from the Project Management Institute.

Security, Audit and Leadership Series

Series Editor: Dan Swanson, Dan Swanson and Associates, Ltd., Winnipeg, Manitoba, Canada.

The scope and mandate for internal audit continues to evolve each year, as does the complexity of the business environment and speed of the changing risk landscape in which it must operate. The fundamental goal of this exciting series is to produce leading-edge books on critical subjects facing security and audit executives and practitioners. Key topics addressed include Leadership, Cybersecurity, Security Leadership, Privacy, Strategic Risk Management, Auditing IT, Audit Management and Leadership, and Operational Auditing.

Integrated Assurance: *Unified Risk Strategy*
By Patrick Hayes

Preparing for Sustainability Audits: *A Practical Guide for IT Sector*
By Mahsa Fidanboy

Scaling Pyramids: *Leadership Lessons from a Mid-Level Bureaucrat*
By Christopher Stitt

Program Architecture: *Fight the Good Fight*
By Gideon T. Rasmussen

Operation Carder Kaos: *How One Agent Penetrated the Underground Community*
By Richard K. LaTulip

Digitalization and Women's Rights: *Women and Sustainability: Volume 2*
By Muharrem Kılıç and Sezer Bozkus Kahyaoglu

Governance, Risk and Compliance: *Demystifying the Risk and Data Privacy Landscape*
By Dr Michael Brass

It's Not in the Manual: *Real-World Leadership for Security and Risk Professionals*
By Michael Gips

Transforming Cybersecurity Audit Practices with Agility and Artificial Intelligence (AI)
By Dr. Linda Kostic

Teach, Train, Transform: *The Superhero Way*
By Denise Cicchella

Audit Alchemy: *Small Teams, BIG Impact – A Guide to Internal Audit Excellence*
By Sandeep Das

Modern Benford's Law: *State of the Art Techniques for Audit and Compliance Professionals*
By Daniel J. McCarville

Modern Benford's Law

State of the Art Techniques for Audit and Compliance Professionals

Daniel J. McCarville

CRC Press
Taylor & Francis Group
Boca Raton London New York

CRC Press is an imprint of the
Taylor & Francis Group, an **informa** business

Designed cover image: Marco Toro Sentado

First edition published 2026
by CRC Press
2385 NW Executive Center Drive, Suite 320, Boca Raton FL 33431

and by CRC Press
4 Park Square, Milton Park, Abingdon, Oxon, OX14 4RN

CRC Press is an imprint of Taylor & Francis Group, LLC

ISBN: 9781032910390 (hbk)
ISBN: 9781032912622 (pbk)
ISBN: 9781003562238 (ebk)

DOI: 10.1201/9781003562238

Typeset in Caslon
by KnowledgeWorks Global Ltd.

Contents

Preface

In 2014, I accepted my first audit role after starting my career in marketing. That same year, an audit manager introduced me to Benford's Law and asked what I thought of it. My response? It sounded counterintuitive and likely had no basis in valid, statistical methods. Little did I know that several years later, I would publish a statistics paper and later, a book on the topic.

This book is intended to bridge the gap between audit practitioners and current research on Benford's Law. Practitioners have access to a wide variety of Benford's Law training materials through professional associations and a wealth of internet blog posts. The vast majority are based on 20+-year-old materials. Unfortunately, scientific research is also generally inaccessible to the audit community. This book is positioned as a "translation" of research into techniques and best practices available to the auditor or compliance professional.

Chapters 1–4 describe fundamentals of using Benford's Law. These chapters should be accessible to anyone without any particular background in statistics, analytics, or technology. They cover the history and description of Benford's Law (Chapter 1), the basic formula and its application (Chapter 2), and a visual library of common results (Chapter 3). Finally, Chapter 4 provides a litany of techniques useful to a practitioner such as the first two-digit test, second-order tests, and more.

Chapters 5–10 describe more advanced methods. These methods all generally require the usage of goodness-of-fit scores, such as the MAD (mean absolute deviation) or D (distance) score. These techniques may require skills in statistics or programming, and so they are generally accessible to audit analytics professionals.

Chapters 11–13 provide supplementary material, which supports the other chapters. Chapter 11 describes professional practice issues such as using Benford's Law at different points during an audit, as well as professional ethics. Chapters 12 and 13 are an extended case study tying together the concepts from other chapters. Finally, the **Appendix** demonstrates how Benford's Law can be derived either algebraically or visually.

Thank you for reading. Writing this book was a labor of love meant to put two different communities – scientists and auditors – in contact. I hope it's as valuable to the reader as it has been to the author.

PART I

Fundamental Approaches to Benford's Law

1

The Story of Benford's Law

Benford's Law is a unique approach to detecting anomalies. In nearly every other form of statistical analysis, numbers are viewed as quantities. One hundred parts in inventory is twice as many as 50 parts. 1,000 employees minus 100 leaves 900. Benford's Law considers only the *digits* and their frequencies. 100 starts with "1." 20 starts with "2." There's no sense that a number starting with "2" is bigger than a number starting with "1." After all, 20 is certainly smaller than 100 despite starting with a bigger digit.

Why do we care? It turns out there is a pattern to these leading digits. This pattern, called Benford's Law, is a useful way to detect anomalies. We typically expect about 30% of numbers to start with "1." If a certain dataset doesn't, we might investigate to find out why. The expected frequency of each digit is in Table 1.1.

Benford's Law has exploded in popularity and usage over the last 30 years. Discovered independently by astronomer Simon Newcomb in 1881 and engineer Frank Benford in 1938, Benford's Law was nothing more than a mathematical brain teaser for almost 100 years. Hal Varian, who would later go on to become the chief economist at

Table 1.1 Frequencies Expected by Benford's Law

LEADING DIGIT	EXPECTED FREQUENCY
1	30.1%
2	17.6%
3	12.5%
4	9.7%
5	7.9%
6	6.7%
7	5.8%
8	5.1%
9	4.6%

DOI: 10.1201/9781003562238-2

Google, first noted its potential to detect fraud in 1972. One hundred years had passed, and there was no extant application of Benford's Law in research or industry.

This changed in the late 1980s. Applications were found in industrial engineering (to test the validity of failure metrics) and financial statement analysis (to detect earnings manipulation). This was the trickle. The dam broke in the 1990s. Mark Nigrini, then a doctoral candidate, used Benford's Law to detect potential income tax evasion in US personal income tax filings. Nigrini would popularize Benford's Law through countless academic papers, professional publications, conference presentations, and more.

Today, the community of Benford's Law users is staggering. It's not limited to accounting or engineering. In fact, those fields make up a small proportion of users. BenfordOnline.net (a resource which collects lists of papers using Benford's Law) indexed 121 new articles in 2023 alone. The uses are mind-boggling.

- Geologists can use Benford's Law to detect earthquakes in seismological data – and even tell the difference between a legitimate earthquake and other sources of disturbances, such as heavy traffic.
- Security analysts can use Benford's Law to discern whether an image is real or AI generated, and whether it's been modified or is an untouched image.
- Medical researchers are able to use Benford's Law to determine whether a patient is properly anesthetized.
- Data scientists have incorporated it into their models, increasing their ability to detect network intrusions, bots in social networks, and more.

The majority of this book will use applications from auditing, compliance, and similar fields. The techniques described will be drawn from the wealth of literature and practice from all disciplines.

1.1 Setting Expectations

What is Benford's Law for? Many auditors have heard of Benford's Law as a fraud detection tool. They use Benford's Law, and it detects something. The auditor gets excited, sets their mind to fraud investigation, and comes up with nothing. They leave disappointed.

Benford's Law is not a fraud detection tool. It's a general-purpose tool for detecting data quality problems including unnatural duplication, rounding, imprecision, missing data, and more. It's a swiss-army knife that is capable of rooting out many different potential problems.

Let's reconsider our hypothetical auditor. They have received a population for testing. They use Benford's Law exactly as before. When their data fails, their mind doesn't jump to fraud. Instead, they focus on understanding why their data doesn't comply. Perhaps they find their transactions have a limit: no transaction is more than $500, and there are *many* transactions just under that limit. The auditor knows that there is a $500 approval limit, so any transaction less than $500 doesn't require outside approval.

Could this be fraud? Certainly, this is a well-known pattern for evading approval thresholds. It's well known both among auditors and in the Benford's Law community. However, people might also attempt to stay under this limit for ordinary, legitimate reasons. The auditor notes this irregularity and proceeds with their audit. They will follow up on this pattern during fieldwork.

Setting expectations made all the difference for these two auditors. One assumed they would find fraud. When they didn't, they got disheartened. They didn't receive any value from their analysis. The second auditor did exactly the same analysis. They will be headed into their audit armed with the knowledge that many transactions are just below the approval threshold. They have smart questions to ask. They're more likely to uncover irregularities worth reporting to management. Even if this isn't an irregularity, they are providing better assurance by being more knowledgeable about their data and their business.

Below are three vignettes demonstrating different uses of Benford's Law.

Example 1 – A Simple Pass or Fail for an ETL Procedure

Olivia is the owner of a batch uploading process for a database. Each month, she receives large extracts from several data sources. She has automated procedures which transform the data and upload it to her database.

She uses Benford's Law as a high-level data quality screening tool. Her automated process saves the new data to a series of temporary staging tables. She uses Benford's Law on the staging tables before allowing it to be saved to the final location. If the data passes, she kicks off the final process, which saves the data to the master, production-ready tables. If the data fails, she performs a series of quality assurance checks to determine if the data is acceptable or should be re-submitted by the user.

Example 2 – Identifying High-Risk Samples

William is an internal auditor in an international firm. He is engaged in an audit of travel and expense claims. He is using data analytics, including Benford's Law, to select individual travel and expense claims to review.

He uses Benford's Law to identify high-risk groups of claims to include in his sample. During the planning of his audit, he heard concerns about specific vendors. He stratifies his data by vendor and uses Benford's Law on each vendor's data. Each vendor is assigned a score to represent how well their data matches Benford's Law. William is able to quickly locate a vendor with a strong deviation from Benford's Law. He includes some transactions from that vendor in his sample.

Example 3 – Tracking Compliance Over Time

Riley is an audit analytics professional developing continuous monitoring tools for their audit team. They build dashboards that track a variety of financial and operational metrics across the enterprise.

They use Benford's Law to monitor data for significant changes. The actual numbers vary a lot month to month (sales are highly seasonal, or operations have a lot of ups and downs). Each month, they test their data against Benford's Law and assign a score representing how well it matches. Their continuous monitoring dashboards show this compliance over time. One month, their score drops: the data suddenly stopped matching Benford's Law. They alert the audit manager, who starts an inquiry to the responsible management team.

1.2 What Does It Mean to "Pass" or "Fail" Benford's Law?

Many people are concerned with whether data "passes" or "fails" Benford's Law. This isn't always the case, and it isn't always useful to think in terms of passing or failing. However, there are enough applications where data passes or fails that we should understand what this means.

Benford's Law is a description of how the first digits of data are distributed. We expect about 30% of numbers to start with "1," about 18% to begin with "2," and so on. When data matches this pattern (or is close enough), we might say it "passes" or "complies" with Benford's Law. When it doesn't, we might say it "fails" or "doesn't comply."

What does this mean to the practitioner? Benford's Law is a description of how numbers are expected to behave if they are natural. "Natural" here is a somewhat philosophical term. There's no precise definition, but generally natural data is:

- Spread over many orders of magnitude, i.e., there are single-digit numbers, two-digit numbers, three-digit numbers, etc.
- The data is spread freely around that whole range. Numbers might be bigger or smaller, but they aren't tightly clustered in a particular place.
- There is no hard maximum or minimum, except 0.
- Numbers are not repeated often.
- The data is complete. There isn't a missing range of data or sub-group.

Each of these topics will be explored in more detail in Chapter 3.

Benford's Law is a useful fraud-detection tool because many fraud schemes will violate these patterns. It's also likely that these patterns will occur for non-fraudulent reasons. For example, numbers may be duplicated because someone is exploiting the accounts payable system by submitting near-duplicate invoices. On the other hand, it could also be that there are recurring purchases that have exactly the same dollar amount. Benford's Law is an alert that something isn't natural. You have to decide what the alert means.

1.2.1 Should My Data Conform to Benford's Law?

Not all data is expected to conform to Benford's Law. This will be covered more in Chapter 2. In short, data that is assigned (such as invoice numbers or zip codes) probably won't follow Benford's Law. In these cases, it's best to use another analytical procedure.

Conforming to Benford's Law isn't always a good thing. Consider the accounts payable example from the prior section. Should disbursements follow Benford's Law? It's true that some kinds of fraud could cause disbursements to fail Benford's Law. Splitting transactions to avoid an approval limit would certainly result in unnatural duplication. It might also result in clustering of results just underneath the approval limit. Benford's Law could detect both of those.

Remember that "natural" means the data should not have an upper or lower limit (except 0). One of the most common controls for accounts payable is to have an approval threshold, where transactions above that threshold require approval (or increasingly strict layers of approval). This creates a soft upper limit on transaction size. An effective approval threshold should make accounts payable data *unnatural* and fail Benford's Law. Many auditors have experienced exactly this problem.

A more colorful example comes from the world of epidemiology. During the COVID-19 pandemic, many people all over the world were closely watching public health reports. These reports commonly summarized the number of COVID-19 cases and deaths. It's no exaggeration to say that 100s of articles were published online by amateur analysts using Benford's Law to argue that their government's COVID-19 data was manufactured. While some manipulation was likely uncovered, this has the same complication as the accounts payable example. Effective public health controls resulted in data that didn't conform to Benford's Law in some areas. The controls placed a soft limit on the spread of disease, which Benford's Law can detect.

1.2.2 Wrapping-Up

Benford's Law is a statistical tool for uncovering data anomalies. "Anomaly" means that the data is unnatural: perhaps it has a limit, plenty of duplication, improper rounding, or something else. Some anomalies result from fraud, noncompliance, or other topics interesting to the auditor. Many other cases are because of the business environment or data quality problems. The auditor needs to use professional judgment to determine why their data fails Benford's Law, and whether it's important to their project.

2
The Basics of Benford's Law

Benford's Law is a mathematical principle that allows us to derive meaning from the leading digits of the records in a dataset. Effectively applying Benford's Law requires that we understand these "significant" digits and know how to extract them from our data. The law predicts the frequency distribution of our digits, revealing how often each should appear in the dataset. By comparing the probabilities expected by Benford's Law to our actual data, we can identify anomalies. Although it's possible to do this through numerical comparison, it is much easier to graph the data and visually identify differences.

2.1 The First-Significant Digit

Benford's Law analyzes *significant digits*. Before we can apply it, we must understand what significant digits are and how they behave. Significant digits (sometimes called "significant figures") are the digits in a number that describe quantity. Leading zeros and trailing zeros are never significant. All other digits carry meaning, making them *significant*.

Consider the number 14. The first digit is 1. 14 is the same number as 014, or 0014, etc. Adding leading zeros doesn't change that the first-significant digit is 1. It's the first digit that conveys meaning. This logic also applies to decimal-value numbers. Consider 0.07. The first-significant digit is 7. Those leading zeros don't convey any quantity. They are just placeholders. Trailing zeros also don't matter: 0.07 is the same as 0.070 or 0.0700. Those extra digits don't add any additional meaning.

Zeros may appear when we are looking at the first two digits (10, 20, 30, etc.). This technique appears in Chapter 4. While a number can never start

DOI: 10.1201/9781003562238-3

with 0, it can start with 10 or 20. In this case, '10' is the first two significant digits even though the zero isn't significant by itself.

2.1.1 *Extracting the First-Significant Digits*

How do we actually extract the first-significant digits from our data? This can be done easily in Excel, Access, SQL, and many other data tools. Be sure to remove currency symbols, negative signs, commas, decimal points, and other non-numeric characters.

An example of an Excel formula that accomplishes this is:

$$\textit{First Significant Digit} = \text{LEFT}\left(\text{ABS}(X * 10000)\right)$$

X is the column from which you want to extract the first digits. Basically, this formula looks at a number and returns the left-most digit. That works in most cases, but there are also numerous edge cases that we may need to account for. For example, a negative number starts with a negative sign ("–") and currency amounts likely start with currency symbols (like "$").

Let's break the formula down a bit:

- X * 10000: This gets rid of small values, so we don't have to worry about decimal points. For example, $0.01 becomes $100 – no more decimal point. If your data is very small (to many decimal places), you may need to multiply by a bigger number.
- ABS(): This is the absolute value. It turns negative numbers into positive numbers, so –100 becomes 100. This removes negative signs from the data.
- LEFT(): This returns the first character. Since we have removed negative values and very small numbers, this will usually be our first digit. By default, LEFT returns the single left-most character. If you wanted to use a first two-digit test, you could instead use LEFT(X, 2) to return the two left-most characters.

As an example, consider the value –$0.007. This is 7/10 of a penny. If this is a number in Excel, the dollar sign is just formatting and won't affect our formulas. Walking through the formula:

- Currently, the left-most character is a negative sign (–). Our first step is to multiply it by 10,000. The new number is –70. There is no longer a decimal place.
- Second, we use the absolute value to turn negative numbers into positive numbers. The new value is 70.
- Finally, we use the LEFT() function to return the left-most character. That is now a '7'.

Your data is likely to have its own special characteristics. Be prepared to modify the formula to meet your needs.

2.1.2 Observing Digit Frequencies

The next step is to count how frequently each digit appears. If you are using Excel, this can be done quickly by using a pivot table. If you are programming a solution (such as in SAS or Python), you will need to use the functions or tools appropriate for your language. An example of digit frequencies for a hypothetical dataset is in Table 2.1.

Since we are looking at the first-significant digit, our expected rows should be the numbers 1–9. If you see 0 or any special characters (such as decimal points, commas, currency symbols, etc.), go back and review your formula. Odds are your data includes some special cases you need to handle.

You have two strategies available: (1) change your data or (2) change your formula. Changing data could mean using Excel's formatting features to remove currency symbols and commas. In a more complicated workflow, it could mean using regular expressions to extract the

Table 2.1 An Example of Observed Frequency of First-Significant Digits

LEADING DIGIT	OBSERVED FREQUENCY
1	28.4%
2	18.2%
3	13.1%
4	9.6%
5	10.3%
6	6.8%
7	6.0%
8	4.6%
9	3.0%

characters you want. For specific guidance, consult a resource dedicated to the tool you are using. Changing your formula means identifying what characteristics it isn't processing and adding additional logic to process those cases.

There is one special value that will need to be handled in almost all cases: the number 0. Since significant digits are defined to be the first non-zero digit, any value that is exactly 0 must be excluded from the analysis. In a pivot table, this is typically as simple as filtering out records that are exactly 0.

2.2 Benford's Law

Benford's Law tells us there is a pattern – or expectation – for how often the first digit should be 1, 2, or any other digit.

Let's call each digit D, where D is any digit 1–9. The probability of the first-significant digit being that number is:

$$Probability\ (D) = log\left(1 + \frac{1}{D}\right)$$

"Log" is the logarithm (in base 10). As an example, the probability of the first-significant digit being 1 is:

$$Probability\ (D=1) = log\left(1 + \frac{1}{1}\right) = log\,(2) = 0.301 \vee 30.1\%$$

Table 2.2 provides the results for all digits 1–9. This same formula can also be used for the expected probability of the first two digits, three digits, etc. This is discussed more in Chapter 4.

Table 2.2 Frequencies Expected by Benford's Law

LEADING DIGIT	EXPECTED FREQUENCY
1	30.1%
2	17.6%
3	12.5%
4	9.7%
5	7.9%
6	6.7%
7	5.8%
8	5.1%
9	4.6%

2.3 Testing Data

We've explored what Benford's Law is, but how does it help us? Well, Benford's Law tells us what to expect in "natural" data – data that hasn't been deliberately altered or constrained. If our data doesn't display the expected pattern, we might question whether it is natural. Perhaps the data is incomplete, or the values have been manipulated. When data deviates significantly from the pattern predicated by Benford's Law, it raises red flags.

What is the expected pattern? In many ways, Benford's Law is an idealized pattern. Real-life data may often be close to that expectation, but may also show marked differences. Chapter 6 discusses an analytical way to handle data that is similar to Benford's Law, but not exactly. Qualitatively, you should expect:

- The first digit ("1" for the first-digit test) is always the most common.
- Every digit has a probability. No digit has 0 records – although some might be very rare.
- Each digit is less common than the one before it. There is no spike or increase at any point.

2.3.1 Plotting the Results

Let's reuse the data from the prior sections. We already have the probabilities for Benford's Law as well as the actual frequencies from our data. You could directly compare these frequencies and observe the differences. However, it's a lot easier using a graph. In this book, we will use a combination chart: bars represent the real data, while the line represents Benford's Law.

Figure 2.1 is an example.

2.3.2 Interpreting the Results

At this point, we should ask ourselves whether the data matches Benford's Law or not. This is a matter of professional judgment. Although many people think of Benford's Law as an analytical test, visual inspection provides a quicker, more intuitive approach that relies on individual experience and interpretation.

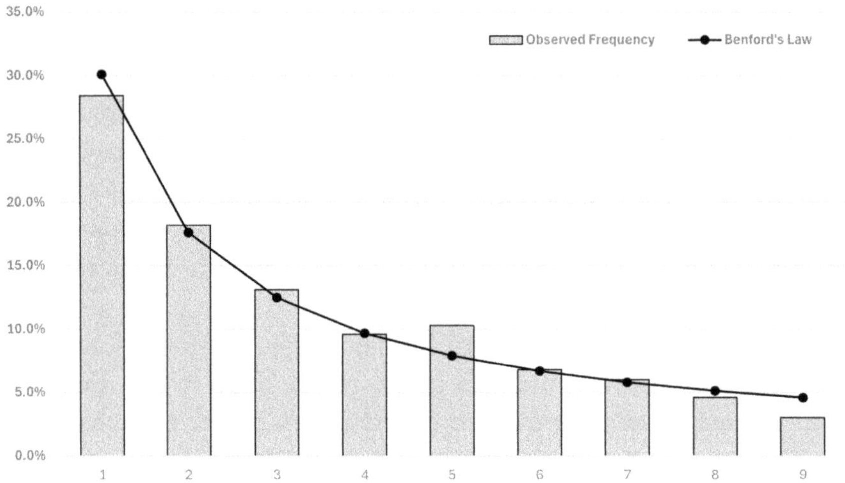

Figure 2.1 Benford's Law compared to first-digit frequencies.

What can we discern from this chart? In some ways, the bars (our data) and the line (Benford's Law) appear similar. The most common first digit is 1, and the chart shows a gradually decreasing curve. However, there are at least two interesting departures from Benford's Law to discern.

- There is a distinct hump or spike at 5. The actual digit frequencies are much larger than expected by Benford's Law.
- The numbers 1 and 9 are less common than expected.

The auditor or analyst may follow up on these patterns. They could dig into the records that start with 5 to see if there are any interesting trends, or they might look for particular subsets of the data that conform better or worse than others. Keep in mind the size of your dataset. Small datasets are easily skewed by random chance. The smaller the dataset, the more likely the spike is just random chance. A spike in a dataset of 30 records is much less concerning that an equally sized spike in a dataset of 3,000 records.

As an example, let's suppose this data represents transactions on someone's personal checking account over a period of two years. The spike at 5 could be explained by a monthly subscription for $51. Alternatively, it could be that a fraudster has been stealing $51 a month and labeling it as a subscription fee. Benford's Law tells us too many transactions start with 5. We must determine whether the reason is legitimate or not.

This is an example of visually inspecting a chart. Examples of common charts and interpretations are included in Chapter 3. The alternative is a statistical or analytical approach, which is more powerful, but requires a bit more know-how. These are covered in the advanced topics beginning in Chapter 5.

2.4 Exceptions to Benford's Law

Not all data is expected to follow Benford's Law. As a quick litmus test, ask yourself:

- Is my data naturally occurring, or was it assigned (such as an invoice number or zip code)?
- Do I have enough data to use Benford's Law?
- Does my data show variation, or are the same numbers being repeated over and over?

Ideally, we assume that our data is in some way random. Numbers that are assigned, such as invoice numbers, IP addresses, zip codes, etc., are not expected to follow Benford's Law. Additionally, we need a certain amount of data to use any kind of data analytics – including Benford's Law. Chapter 5 addresses this in more detail. If you have a dataset of hundreds or thousands of records (or more!), you can use the single-digit test.

Similarly, uniformly distributed data does not follow Benford's Law. Random number generators are a common example – since digits are expected to be equally likely, we can't use Benford's Law to test whether the generator is working. There are other analytical tests, such as the Kolmogorov-Smirnov test, which can accomplish this goal.

Data requires a meaningful variety in order to use Benford's Law. A large amount of repeating values will almost certainly be detected. This is often a problem for machine learning models using imputed values. The imputed values are often heavily repeated, so we can't use Benford's Law on those columns. This can also occur in inventory records, asset listings, and other populations with lots of repetition.

Traditional auditor wisdom says that the data should span many orders of magnitude for Benford's Law to apply. For example, accounting data should have transactions that are one digit ($5), two digits ($50), three digits ($500), up to thousands or millions of dollars to logically apply the law. Mathematically, that just isn't true. Even data distributed between $0.01 and $0.09 could follow Benford's Law. However, for practical (and non-mathematical) reasons, it often does work best when the data spans at least a few orders of magnitude.

Another common belief is that auditors must stratify their transactions before using Benford's Law. Various experts claim that you should stratify credits and debits, exclude transactions below $1, or transactions below $100. There is no mathematical or statistical reason to do this. Feel free to mix credits and debits (or positive and negative numbers) and include your entire population. Always rely on your subject-matter knowledge. If you know that credits are processed differently from debits, then you should use good professional judgment when constructing your population.

3
Common Results – with Graphs

Visual analysis is a useful, but often inconclusive, tool. It's less science and more art. The user must be able to interpret the graph and understand what is happening with their data. Despite these challenges, visual analysis is useful as a quick and intuitive way to evaluate data. Many potential errors can be spotted simply by looking at the chart without the need for more robust analytical procedures.

Analysis is also much quicker when you already know the pattern to look for. Exploratory analysis (where the end goal is unknown) is a great tool in the auditor's toolkit. However, knowing in advance what pattern you expect to find greatly speeds up the analysis. This chapter presents several common patterns and explains how to interpret each one. Each example includes potential explanations. In practice, the auditor will need to think about their data and potentially investigate more to decide what each pattern means in their particular situation.

3.1 The Classic Example: Avoiding a Limit

Probably the most well-known example of Benford's Law is using it to detect some kind of limit-avoiding behavior. There are many variations. For example, purchases often have approval thresholds. These could be hard thresholds (like a card that doesn't allow purchases over a certain value) or soft thresholds (such as requiring approval for transactions above a certain value). Reporting obligations, compliance requirements, monitoring flags, and more might all be based on thresholds.

Figure 3.1 shows an example that could indicate someone trying to avoid a limit. If the limit is phrased as "transactions $1,000 or more

DOI: 10.1201/9781003562238-4

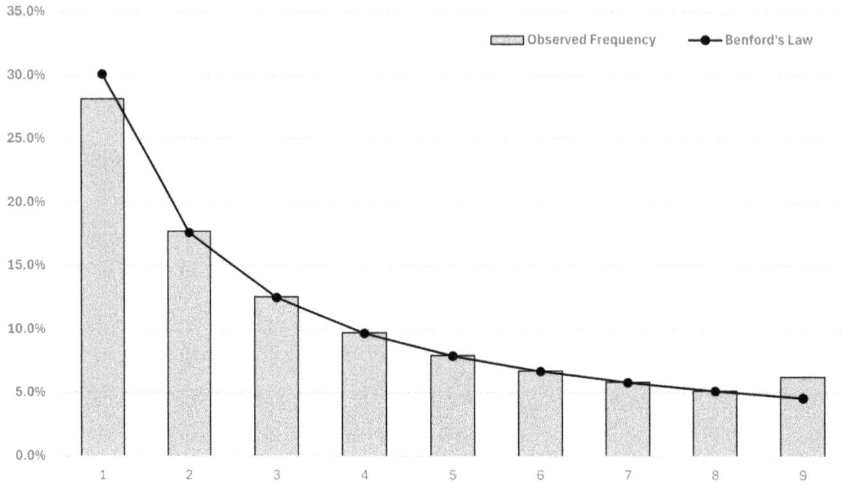

Figure 3.1 Example of transactions coming under a threshold at "1."

require approval," we might expect to see lots of transactions *just under* $1,000 – say, in the $900 range. Our chart would have too many "9's" and too few "1's."

This same pattern could occur at any digit. If the approval threshold were $300, we would expect transactions to be in the $200 range. The pattern would be the same: too few transactions where the limit is ("3") and too many transactions just below it ("2").

You could also have a lower limit. Sales data might have a bias toward reporting larger values. Revenue values in financial statements suffer from the same problem. Consider a situation where management wants to report strong revenue figures. They could have a bias to report a "big" number like $10 million instead of the "smaller" number like $9.9 million. A fraudulent financial statement could unfairly round those numbers up. Figure 3.2 shows this reversed pattern: there could be too many transactions that start with "1" (the limit) and too few just below it.

There are mundane reasons this could show up too. People may avoid limits for non-fraudulent reasons. For example, to avoid the extra paperwork that comes with compliance. They could also avoid limits for purely psychological reasons such as feeling anxious by larger purchases.

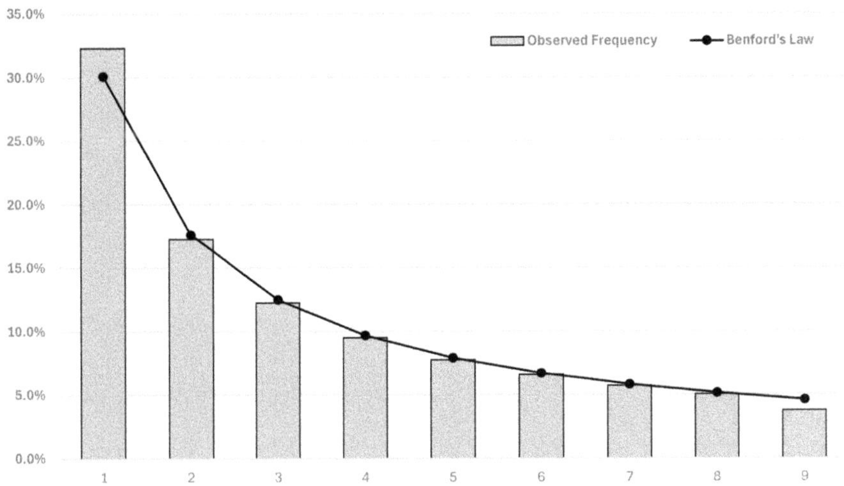

Figure 3.2 Example of transactions coming over a threshold at "1."

3.2 Missing Data

Operational data sometimes suffers from data missing either very small or very large values. For example, IT may fail to record interruptions of a cloud-based service if the interruptions are very small. Delivery drivers may fail to report small delays. Alternatively, very large events may evade being recorded because they are considered unusual.

Benford's Law can help detect these scenarios. Consider the chart below. The data shows a spike at "4." A reader could imagine this is a case of avoiding a limit (see Section 3.1). What makes it different is that there is a change in the graph at "4." Before "4," all the digits are less common than Benford's Law expects. After "4," they are all normal. That's our clue that something special happened at "4."

What happened? There is data missing. In this case, data started being recorded at 40. There is data missing from 0 to 39, creating the visual pattern in Figure 3.3. A fuller example of this pattern is explored with the first two-digit test in Chapter 4.

This pattern sometimes occurs legitimately when the business process under review doesn't include data in some range. For example, consider an analysis of tractor sales. New tractors for agricultural use might start around $25,000. There could appear to be "missing" data from $1 to $24,999. In practice, if we have enough data, and that

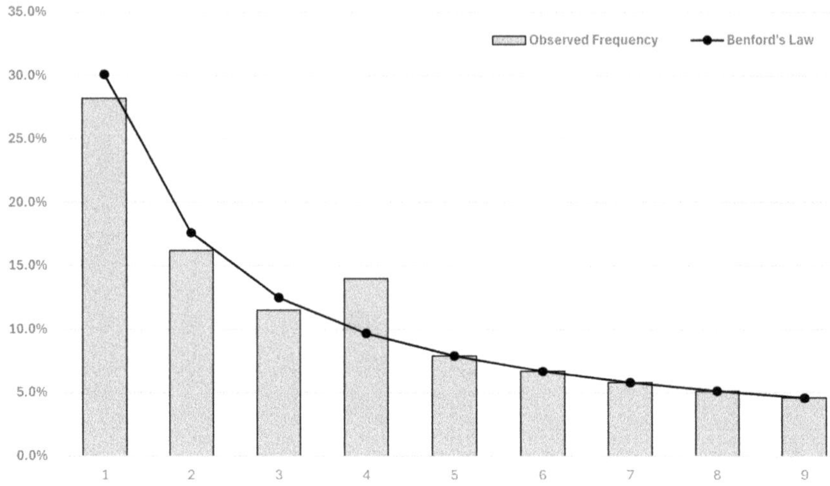

Figure 3.3 Example of missing data between 1 and 3.

data covers many orders of magnitude (perhaps reaching hundreds of thousands or millions of dollars), the impact is often reduced.

3.3 Spikes and Potential Duplicate Transactions

This is probably the most common result in many kinds of data. A single digit has a very large spike, and all other digits are below Benford's Law. It's not uncommon to see a single digit representing 60% in some cases. The cause is usually that many records have similar values (either identical or just close to each other).

The fraudulent case would be either duplicate transactions or that a fraudster has determined a safe range of transactions for their scheme. A more mundane (and common) explanation is that the transactions or records have consistent values. This can still be an interesting case to pursue.

Consider an example I've seen on multiple travel and expense card audits. Figure 3.4 shows the digit frequencies from an analysis of travel and expense claims. The auditors used Benford's Law and found several employees who showed 70% or more in the "1" digit. That's a clear spike – a deviation from Benford's Law. They discovered the employees had software subscriptions on their T&E cards.

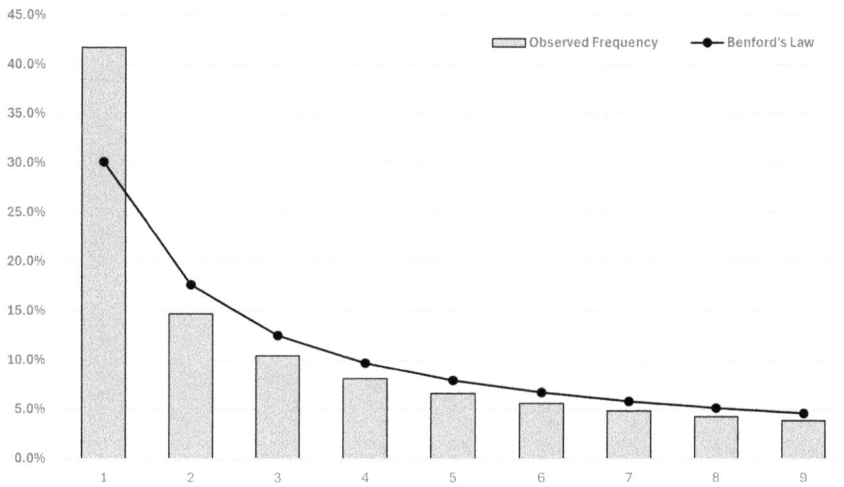

Figure 3.4 Example of duplicate or reoccurring payments.

The transactions weren't fraudulent duplicate payments, but recurring payments of exactly the same amount. Although it isn't fraud, it's still worthwhile to know. Many organizations' policies prohibit these kinds of expenses on T&E cards. Even if it's allowed, it may raise other questions surrounding effective AP management and third-party risk management of software vendors.

This pattern is different from the prior two. It's different from the pattern for avoiding a limit, because that pattern only changed two digits: one is too high, one is too low. In this pattern, one digit is too high and all the others are too low. The data is essentially concentrated in a single digit. It's also different from missing data, which only reduced the frequency in a certain set of missing digits.

3.4 Imprecise or Estimated Data

Data may suffer from imprecision. This occurs when the data is approximately true, but is inexact. For example, if we asked controllers for the dollar value of revenues, their answers would be in the right ballpark (on average), but wouldn't match the financial statements exactly. This may occur any time we are asking people to provide numbers in surveys, interviews, and other scenarios.

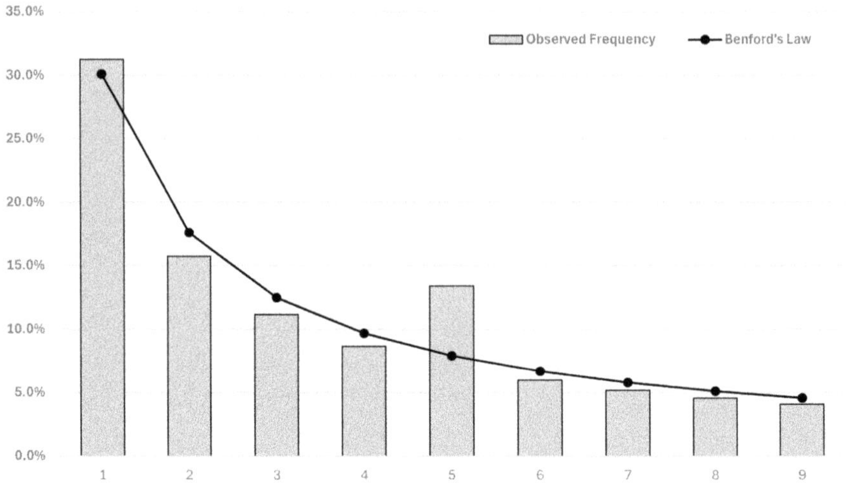

Figure 3.5 Example of imprecise or estimated data.

Benford's Law detects this kind of imprecision.[1] Humans have a bias toward numbers that start with "1" or "5." Imagine you spent $94.21 on groceries. If your partner asked how much you spent, what would you say? Would you provide the exact amount? Most people would say something like "about $100." The result is that we see too many "1's" and "5's," but too few other digits. Figure 3.5 provides an example of this pattern.

Although the first two-digit test hasn't been introduced yet, this pattern can also be detected with that technique. See Chapter 4 for additional details on the first two-digit test.

3.5 Data with Limits

There are two types of limits: hard and soft. Hard limits exist when *no* data exists beyond the limit. Soft limits exist when very little data exists past a limit. In either case, when data suddenly becomes sparse after a certain point, it almost definitely fails Benford's Law.

Figures 3.6 and 3.7 illustrate these kinds of limits. In both cases, there is a limit at "3." The results show plenty of data from 1 to 3, then a sudden drop-off:

Figure 3.6 is an example of a hard limit. There are 0 records that start with "4"–"9." Typically, this happens when the data only covers a small

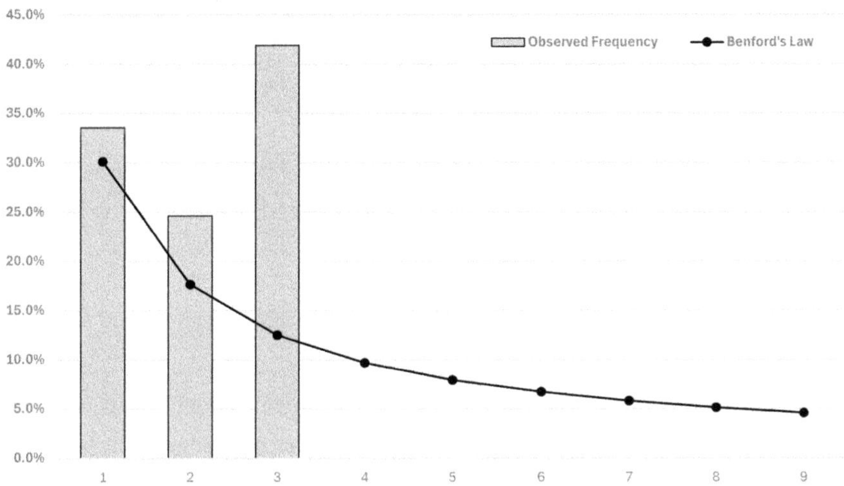

Figure 3.6 Example of data with a hard limit.

range. For example, if this data only ran from $100 to $350 there is no chance that it could have a number starting with "9." This example shows a spike on "3." This often happens with limits, but not always. It's possible you might see a clean curve that suddenly drops off.

Figure 3.7 has some data in "4"–"9," but very little. In this case, the data at least has the possibility of starting with each digit. Consider

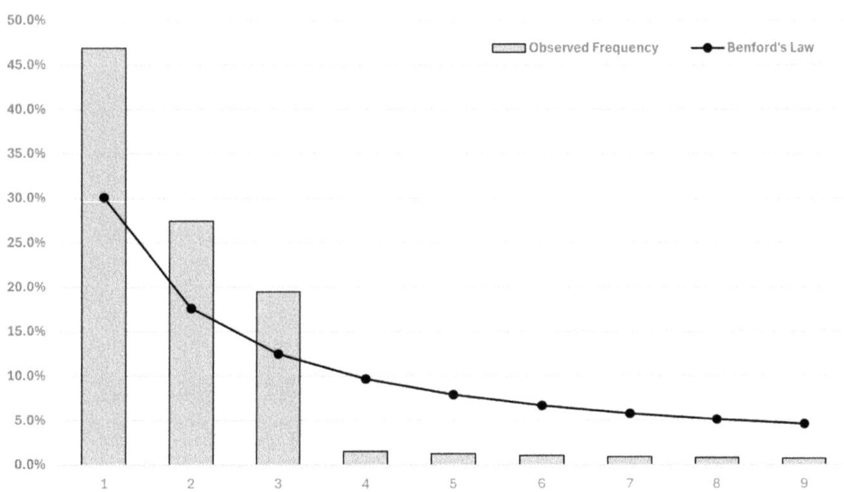

Figure 3.7 Example of data with a soft limit.

transactions under $25 (perhaps travel expenses under a $25 receipt requirement). It's possible for there to be a transaction that starts with any digit, but the digits "1" (covering $10–$19) and "2" (covering $20–$25) are the most likely.

Data transformation can be used to "stretch" data and remove these limits. The result is a distribution that matches Benford's Law better. Data transformation is covered in Chapter 4.

3.6 Not Enough Data

Like any kind of analysis, Benford's Law requires a certain amount of data to provide meaningful results. If you are using a score (such as the D-Score or MAD, which are introduced in chapter 6), there might be a statistical way to decide how much data you need. Otherwise, it's professional judgment. There are a variety of recommendations between a hundred and several thousand records.

If you don't have enough data, your chart will appear erratic. Some digits will be too common, some too uncommon. There's no pattern for the highs and lows. It's erratic, because there's not enough data for a coherent pattern to emerge. Figure 3.8 is an example.

There's a trade-off here. More records mean your data is less erratic. You won't see false positives just from bad luck. On the other hand,

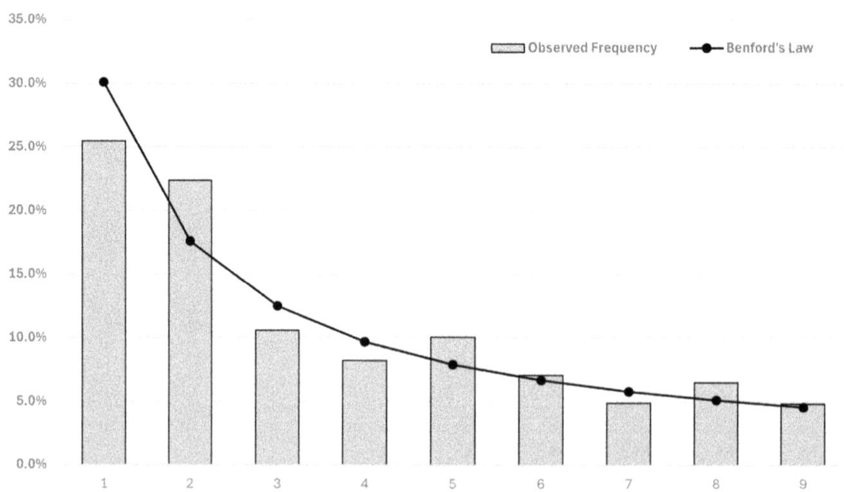

Figure 3.8 Example of erratic results.

more data means you become less able to spot small frauds and errors. If you have one million records, thousands might have to be erroneous or fraudulent to visibly change your chart.

Note

1. This pattern was first observed by George Judge at the University of California-Berkeley and Laura Schector at the University of Wisconsin. They analyzed self-reported agricultural data and found the values were imprecise using Benford's Law. You can read their article "Detecting Problems in Survey Data with Benford's Law" in the *Journal of Human Resources.*

4
Intermediate Topics

The first-digit test presented in Chapter 2 is the most common approach to Benford's Law. This chapter presents a handful of other approaches such as the two-digit test and the second-order test. These techniques don't involve more sophisticated mathematics, but they do require a basic understanding of Benford's Law. Readers who feel comfortable with the earlier chapters should explore this chapter without fear.

This chapter also marks a transition between the basic approach to Benford's Law and the advanced techniques presented in future chapters. You might need to be a little bit more data-savvy to apply these, but you don't require any specific mathematical or programming skills. These techniques become even more powerful when combined with the advanced techniques.

4.1 Two-Digit Test

The first-digit test used in Chapter 2 uses only the first digit of each number. The two-digit test uses the first two. Using two digits provides a more granular look into our data. We can see more precise areas where things may be wrong. For example, the first digit "1" might look overall fine. On further inspection, we may see that "19" is far too frequent. This could indicate that people are trying to avoid hitting "20" – a common pattern if there is an approval limit or other control at that point.

There are some well-known patterns that are observable in the two-digit test. For example, in financial data, it's common to see spikes at numbers that end in "0" and "5" such as \$100, \$105, \$110, \$115, etc. This is usually for psychological reasons, but at times can indicate an auditable interest. Similarly, unfairly rounded transactions could result in a high number of records in 10, 20, 30, etc.

 DOI: 10.1201/9781003562238-5

4.1.1 Formula for the Two-Digit Test

The formula for the two-digit test is exactly like the formula for the single-digit test:

$$Probability\ (D) = log\left(1+\frac{1}{D}\right)$$

D is the digit you are interested in. The only difference between the single-digit and two-digit test is that D is now a two-digit number. For example, the probability of transactions expected to start with "21" (i.e., \$21, \$2.10, \$0.21, etc.) is:

$$Probability(21) = log\left(1+\frac{1}{21}\right) = log\,(1.048) = about\ 2\%$$

Benford's Law for the first two digits is depicted in Figure 4.1. The same process can be used to analyze any number of digits (i.e., the first three digits, first four digits, etc.). Benford's Law is generally not used to analyze anything besides the first digits. For example, it shouldn't be used to analyze the second digit, the third digit, the last digit, etc. It's possible, but not easy (and often not worth the work).

The first-digit test is sufficient for most cases, but the two-digit test also has attractive qualities. The most important is that the two-digit test is more detailed. It might reveal detailed patterns that the first-digit test obscures. For example, a key monitoring control which applies to database connections might only start when a connection's lifespan exceeds a certain length, like 240 seconds (4 minutes). This might not be obvious on the first digit test, since the overall frequency of the digit "2" might be close to the expectation. The two-digit test would show too many observations at "22" or "23," but too few at "24" and above.

The two-digit test also comes with downsides. There are many more digits to analyze. The first-digit test only has 9 digits. The two-digit test has 90 possible digits (10–99). Your result will be a bar chart with 90 bars. That's a lot of visual information to take in. Since there are more bars, the results also tend to be "noisier": some bars will go up and down with relatively little explanation. It's best not to get bogged down in details, but look for trends in terms of what is higher or lower than expected. This noise can be reduced with a larger data set. It's often

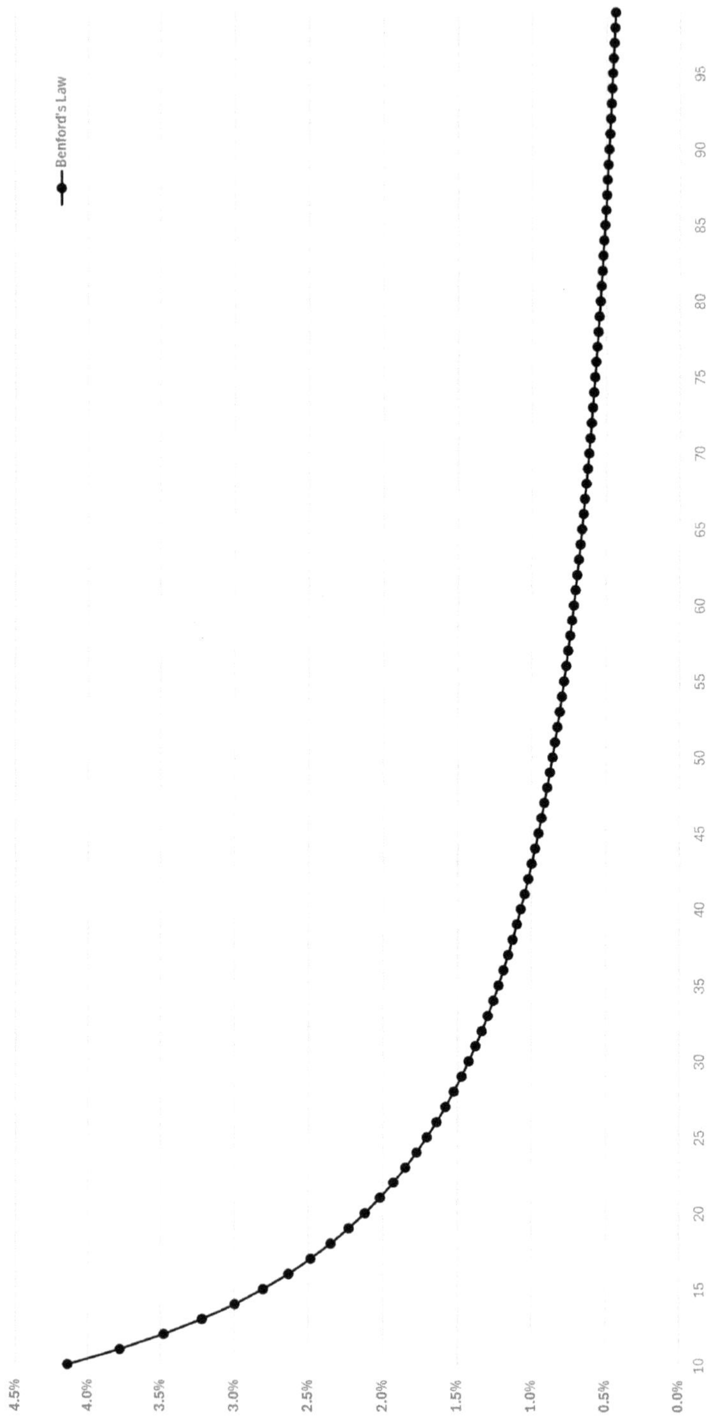

Figure 4.1 Benford's Law for two digits.

possible to use the single-digit test with 100 or more records. To successfully use the two-digit test, you should have thousands of records.

4.2 Example Application: Greenhouse Gas Emissions

The US Environmental Protection Agency requires certain facilities to report their greenhouse gas emissions each year.[1] Consider an auditor examining this greenhouse gas emissions data. In 2023, about 7,500 facilities reported their emissions. All emissions are measured in metric tonnes of CO_2. Figure 4.2 shows the first-digit test.

There seems to be a pattern here. There are too few "1's," and too many in the "2"–"4" range. This pattern could indicate a lower limit that is filtering out facilities that would have emissions starting with "1." Let's use the two-digit test to get a more detailed view. Figure 4.3 visualizes the frequency of the first two digits.

The two-digit test results in many more columns. That can be overwhelming. How can an auditor keep track of what's happening in all these columns? Don't worry about each individual spike. Spikes can be produced by random chance. The mathematics of this is covered more in Chapter 5's discussion of Z-scores, but on average, the two-digit test will contain 5 false positives. That means 5 columns that have unusually large values due to random chance alone.

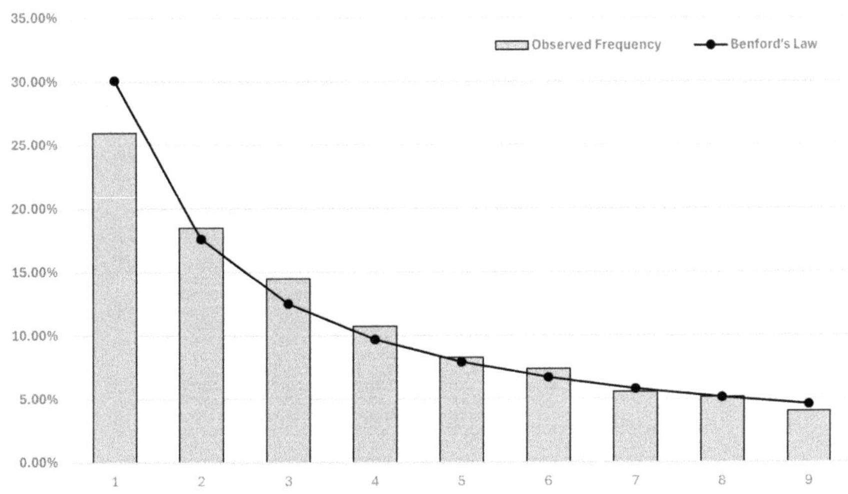

Figure 4.2 First-digit test for EPA greenhouse gas emissions data.

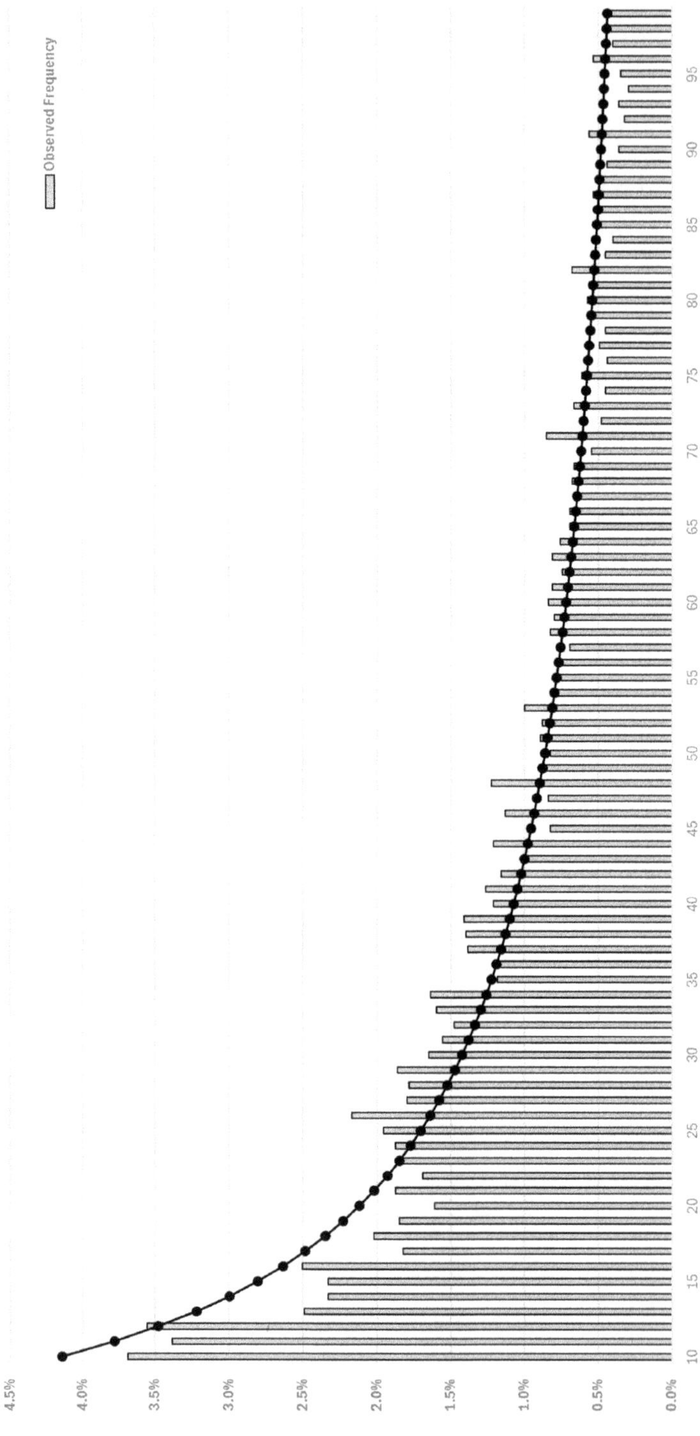

Figure 4.3 Two-digit test for EPA greenhouse gas emissions data.

As an example, look at the column for "71." Benford's Law expects 0.61% of records to start with "71." The actual data is significantly higher at 0.88%. Manually reviewing the records starting with "71" doesn't reveal any obvious pattern or story. One option would be to ask for subject-matter experts in sustainability or emissions to review the data. For most audits, this would not be an efficient use of resources. It's more effective to focus our attention on areas where there are indicators of risk.

There are still some reasons to focus on individual columns. First, if the spike is large enough, it may be worthwhile to look. Although statistically meaningful, this spike is not particularly dramatic. Second, if the spike appears in an area that is meaningful to the topic, it should be investigated. For example, if there was an approval control at $1,000 and the data had a large spike at "99," we should be concerned.

The two-digit test includes so many columns that it's more effective to focus on patterns. Look for ranges that are consistently too low or too high. In this case, "10"–"22" are nearly all too low. The neighboring range of "24"–"34" is too frequent. Next, manually review records in the range of "24"–"34." It's often not useful to review the range with missing data, because it's hard to understand data we can't see.

Manually reviewing the data reveals a pattern: although there are a few records with very small emissions, most facilities start around 23,000 metric tonnes. Starting around 25,000 metric tonnes the number of records starts growing quickly. What's going on here? The regulations surrounding who is required to report greenhouse gases are complex and vary by the kind of facility. However, a broad generalization is that for many facilities reporting requirements kick-in at 25,000 metric tonnes.

GHGRP has a soft floor at 25,000 metric tonnes. There is *some* data below this threshold, but fairly little. This floor is based on reporting regulations. Benford's Law identifies this floor. Is this important? If the auditor wasn't already aware of this reporting requirement, then Benford's Law was successful in identifying an interesting trait. If the auditor was already aware of this requirement, then they have learned something interesting about the behavior of the data. It's unlikely this pattern represents fraud or error, but it's something to keep in mind. Soft limits can be challenging because there is some data both above and below the limit (in this case, 25,000 metric tonnes).

4.3 Second-Order Test

Sometimes data doesn't follow Benford's Law. One solution is to use a second-order test.[2] In this analysis, we sort the data, calculate the difference between each item, and use Benford's Law on that. The second-order test is useful in several different scenarios:

- Data without much variation. For example, thermometers or other sensor readings might have readings that are very close together (68.214, 68.627, 67.665, etc.). These numbers obviously don't follow Benford's Law, because they all start with "6."
- Data where the order of observations is important. For example, when data is streaming through an API, sensor, or other solution, the order of each value may be important. Second-order tests look at the change between values coming in, not just their overall distribution.
- Distributions that clearly don't follow Benford's Law. For example, if our data was distributed between $100 and $250 (perhaps these are travel & expense card purchases subject to specific limits), it wouldn't follow Benford's Law.

Table 4.1 contains a simple illustration showing these calculations. We would use Benford's Law to examine the new column, which contains the differences between rows. The idea is that the data is highly consistent, but those differences display all the traits we want to use Benford's Law.

There are mathematical proofs that establish that Benford's Law can be used on the differences between data sets. There are conditions on those proofs, but they are the kinds of things that are of interest to mathematicians rather than audit and compliance professionals.

Table 4.1 Example of Second-Order Test Calculations

SENSOR READING	DIFFERENCE (THIS ROW MINUS THE ABOVE ROW)	FIRST DIGIT
9.21568	–	N/A
9.5159	0.3002	3
9.7159	0.2000	2

How do we apply this technique?

1. Sort your data. Order matters because we are looking at the differences between rows. The two most common approaches to sorting are either to sort high-to-low or in chronological order. Sorting high-to-low is generally appropriate. Chronological order can be appropriate for streaming data (such as from IoT devices, physical sensors, or transactional IT systems).
2. Calculate the difference between each row and the preceding row. You won't be able to calculate this for the first row, since nothing precedes it.
3. Find the first-significant digit of each row. Remember, 0 is never the first-significant digit.
4. Use Benford's Law like normal.

The main challenge to this approach is that it's hard to interpret the end result. If the number "5" is high, that doesn't mean there are too many records that start with "5." It means that there are many cases where two records are spaced "5" apart (perhaps 5, 0.5, or 0.05 apart). It still fails Benford's Law, but it's hard to know what to do with that information.

4.4 Example Application: Fleet Mileage

Consider an audit of a fleet of company vehicles. The dataset includes several thousand records representing trips made using a company vehicle. Each record identifies the distance (in miles) of each trip. A simple first-digit test (as described in Chapter 2) results in Figure 4.4. There are far too many "1's" and a small bump at "9." Although we haven't discussed scoring datasets yet (see Chapter 5), this data has a D-score of 7.4: overwhelmingly non-compliant.

This result tells us that too many mileages start with "1." Unfortunately, after browsing the data, it isn't clear exactly what the problem is. A mundane explanation would be that the locations our teams often visit are roughly 1 mile or 10 miles apart. Let's try the second-order test instead.

The first step is to sort our data. For this example, we will sort by the distance column itself. Then, create a new column and calculate

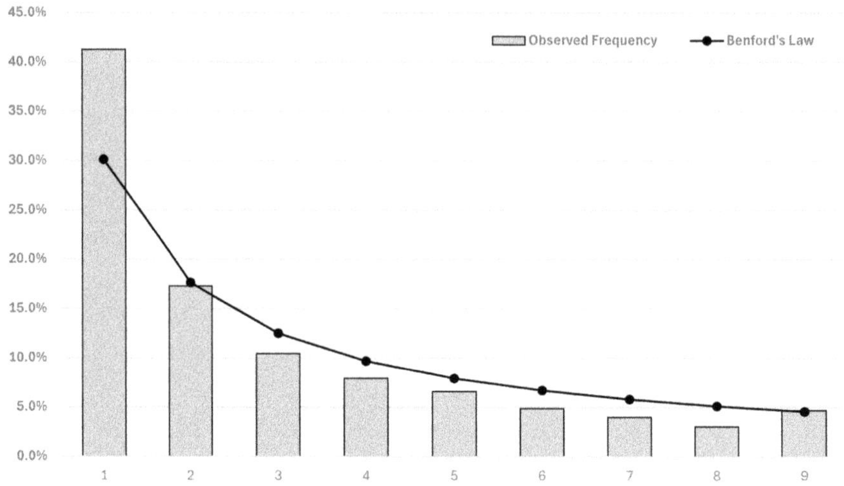

Figure 4.4 First-significant digit for trip mileage.

the difference between each distance and the distance before it. One interesting property of this approach is that it removes duplicate distances (since the difference of two duplicate distances will be 0, which doesn't have a first-significant digit).

The second-order test results in Figure 4.5. Now this is a much clearer story! About 60% of the records start with "1"! Remember,

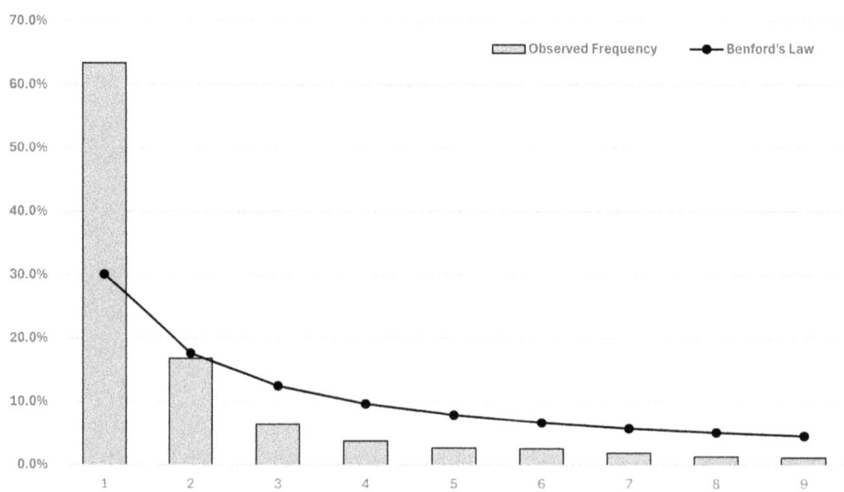

Figure 4.5 Second-order test on trip mileage.

that doesn't mean the distance of each trip starts with "1." It means that the difference between two trips starts with "1." What does this mean? By visually inspecting some records, the root cause became clear: nearly all of these records have a difference of 0.01 miles. The data is being rounded to the nearest 0.01 mile when it's recorded.

Is that okay? That depends on the context. In many audit contexts, this may not be especially important. However, there are many cases where rounded data may be a problem such as when statutory, regulatory, or contractual requirements are more precise. For example, if the contract with the client requires billing for every 0.05 mile rounding to the nearest 0.1 mile would be inadequate (and potentially fraudulent!). Detecting a statistical irregularity is only the beginning. The auditor always needs to consider whether that irregularity is interesting for their project.

4.5 Changing Scales

Benford's Law is scale invariant: data that follows Benford's Law in one scale (like US dollars) still follows Benford's Law when converted to another scale (like Icelandic krona). This property doesn't come up often, but it has some utility when data is getting translated between different scales. One common example is an ERP for an international company which translates currencies automatically. Benford's Law won't be challenged by those currency conversions, or even mixed currencies.

Data is always measured on some kind of scale. A simple example would be measuring the height of a person. We could use meters, inches, feet, rods, or some other unit. These units of measure are the scale. The most common example for most auditors is measuring the size of a transaction in US dollars, euros, yen, or some other currency.

Benford's Law is *scale invariant*. This just means that changing the scale doesn't change how well a dataset fits Benford's Law. If you have a large dataset with transactions in US dollars that follows Benford's Law, it should still follow Benford's Law if you translate the currency to South Korean won. Data that didn't follow Benford's Law still won't follow Benford's Law.

The simplest example occurs when converting between scales involves multiplying by 10, 100, etc. For example, natural gas can be measured in many different units. Common units include CCF (hundred cubic feet) and MCF (thousand cubic feet). 10 CCF = 1 MCF. Translating between CCF and MCF never changes the first digit. A facility that used 10 CCF of natural gas used 1 MCF: both start with "1." A facility that used 84.1 CCF used 8.41 MCF: both start with 8.

There are two notable exceptions. First, the dataset must be meaningfully large. A small dataset can be noisy. It might fit better or worse due to random chance. This risk is ameliorated with a larger dataset. Second, rounding can sometimes introduce errors into this process. Let's reconsider the natural gas example. A small office could allocate natural gas usage among several smaller tenants. Suppose an individual tenant only consumed 7 CCF of natural gas. That is 0.7 MCF. A utility company rounding to the nearest whole unit would report 1 MCF. Benford's Law would likely be violated by this rounding process.

4.6 Data Transformation

Another solution to dealing with tightly clustered or consistent data is to transform the data. *Transform* means we will modify the values to be something Benford's Law can handle. A common example of data transformation is converting between currencies. If 1 USD = 0.90 EUR, we can transform our USD to EUR by multiplying our USD × 0.90. Easy.

There is an established data transformation procedure for Benford's Law. We can take data that doesn't fit Benford's Law and change its shape by taking every value to the tenth power. That is, for every row (let's call it X), replace it with x^{10}. Use Benford's Law as normal on the new values. The idea here is that we are "stretching" the data to cover many orders of magnitude. Data that used to be very close together have now been stretched out, so we have data from all the digits now represented. Table 4.2 provides a simple example.

Data transformation is useful, but has a significant limitation: interpretation. It's much more difficult to interpret the results of Benford's Law after using data transformation. Normally, we can substantively understand the "story" of an issue by looking at the results of Benford's Law. If there are too many transactions starting with "7," we might consider whether there is an approval threshold at "8" or perhaps duplicate values in that range. Data transformation removes this interpretation. What do we do when the transformed values have too many "7's"? They could have originally started with any digit!

Table 4.2 Transforming Records by Raising Them to the 10th Power

SENSOR READING	TRANSFORMED VALUE
9.21568	4.4 billion
9.5159	6.1 billion
9.7159	7.5 billion

Note that our data used to all have the same first digit (9). The transformed data has a variety of different first digits (4, 6, and 7). For small numbers (like the table above) even a small difference in the value can produce an entirely different first digit in the transformed value. For much larger numbers, additional variance may be necessary to properly cover all digits.

Transformation allows us to salvage Benford's Law analyses that otherwise would be impossible. The results are somewhat limited: we can tell that the data do (or do not) conform to Benford's Law, but following up on the results is difficult. All analytical choices come with tradeoffs.

4.7 Example Application: Accounts Payable Amounts

Consider an audit of accounts payable. The audit team is looking at the expenditures for a single vendor. Although transactions for a single vendor *might* follow Benford's Law, often it doesn't. Figure 4.6 shows the first-digit test for the vendor's data.

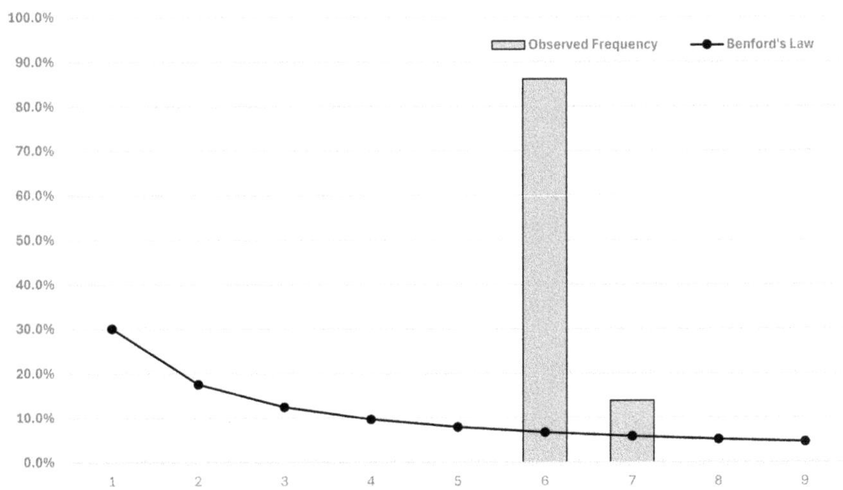

Figure 4.6 Transaction amounts for a single vendor.

The data doesn't span all the digits: all of the transactions start with "6" or "7." That's a clue. It's likely the data covers only a small range. Indeed, visually inspecting the accounts payable records shows that transactions are all between $600 and $720. Many kinds of vendors display this kind of consistency. The vendor could have a monthly fixed fee plus a variable amount based on utilization. It could be a service-based vendor where our variable costs are highly consistent. In any case, Benford's Law analysis isn't very useful.

Data transformation can help us extract more value from our analysis. For each transaction, we will raise the price to the tenth power. This will result in much longer numbers. That's okay. For each of those new, longer, prices, we will take the first digit. The results are in Figure 4.7. The data isn't a perfect fit for Benford's Law, but it's much better. The data now spans nearly all digits, and the overall pattern is a clean, sloping curve.

Why doesn't the data match perfectly? One interpretation could be that the vendor has some kind of meaningful deviation from Benford's Law. Typically, Benford's Law doesn't like hard limits (minimums or maximums). This vendor's data had both: it started at $600 and ended at $720. If the vendor's transaction had reached just a little higher, around $750, there could have been transactions where the transformed values started with "4" or "5." An additional

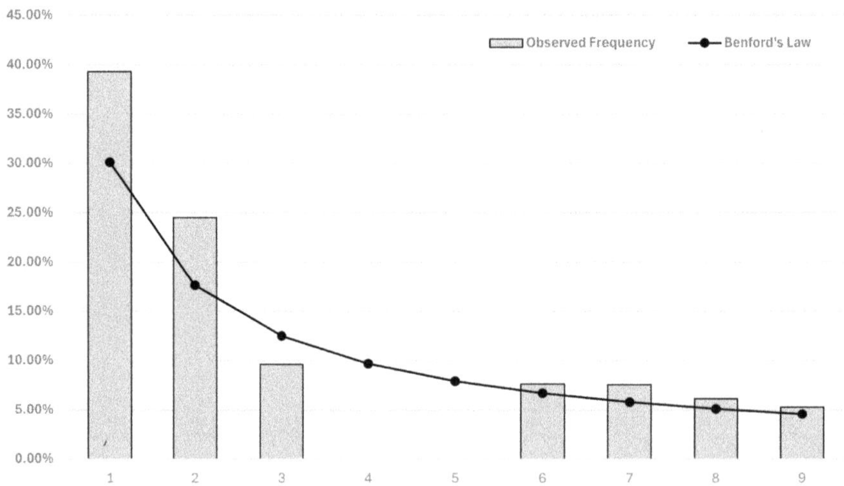

Figure 4.7 Transactions for single vendor after transformation.

consideration is the number of transactions. This vendor had several thousand, but a smaller dataset could have suffered from having too few records.

This also highlights the major challenge with data transformation. It's hard to substantively understand the nature of the deviation. What does it mean that the transformed digits don't start with "4" or "5"? Unfortunately, we can't say: the transformed values don't have clear interpretations. Using the transformation procedure gave a clearer statistical answer, but reduced our ability to interrogate the results.

This technique is especially powerful when combined with some of the advanced topics presented later. For example, we could perform this same analysis with every vendor in the population. We could calculate a score to tell us which vendors were closer or farther from Benford's Law. Finally, we could transform the data to get rid of false positives for vendors with highly consistent transactions like this one.

4.8 Generating Random Benford's Law-compliant Data

Normally, auditors use Benford's Law to analyze organizational data. In some cases, it may be important to generate random numbers which satisfy Benford's Law.[3] Thankfully, generating these numbers (called "variates") is relatively easy. It can be done with two columns in Excel. The general process involves two steps:

1. Generate random numbers between 0 and 1. In Excel, this can be easily done with the RAND() function. Python, SQL, Alteryx, and other tools have their own functions for accomplishing this.
2. For each random number (n) calculate 10^n.

The resulting values will follow Benford's Law. Table 4.3 demonstrates these calculations.

Figure 4.8 shows the results for a dataset of 5,000 random numbers generated using this process. The results are almost identical to Benford's Law.

Creating this figure is a fantastic exercise for developing statistical reasoning skills. Each time the random numbers are

Table 4.3 Generating Random Numbers that Follow Benford's Law

N: RANDOM NUMBER BETWEEN 0 AND 1	10^N: NUMBER FOLLOWING BENFORD'S LAW
0.066	1.165
0.971	9.355
0.071	1.179
0.358	2.281
0.843	6.966
0.211	1.625
0.993	9.840
0.876	7.508
0.201	1.589
0.936	8.623

created, the result changes. In fact, often the results will be visibly different from Benford's Law! This is a simple product of randomness. Try generating datasets of different sizes (100 records, 1,000 records, or 10,000 records) and observe how difficult it is to get a dataset that matches Benford's Law. Try refreshing the data in Excel (by making a change to any cell) and watch the random numbers fluctuate.

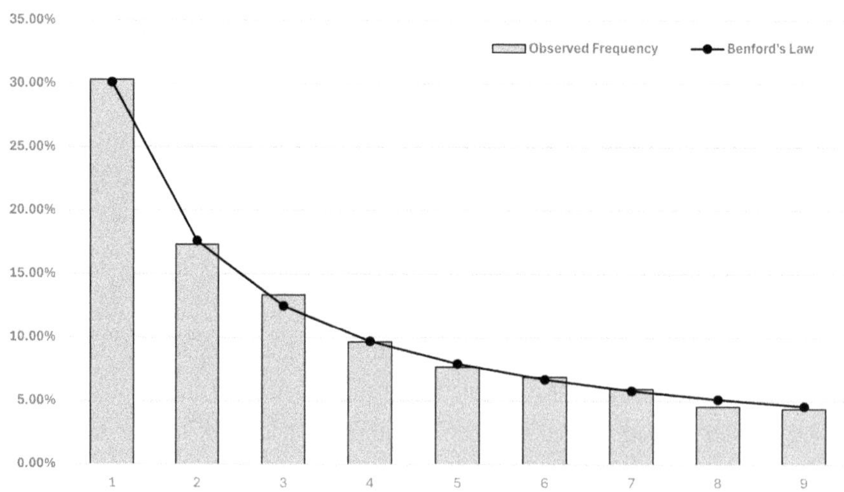

Figure 4.8 5,000 randomly generated numbers following Benford's Law.

Notes

1. This is the EPA's Greenhouse Gas Reporting Program (GHGRP). GHGRP data can be downloaded from the EPA's website: http://ghgdata.epa.gov/ghgp. This analysis is based on all 2023 emissions reported.
2. The second-order test was first published by Mark Nigrini at the College of New Jersey and Steven Miller at Williams College. See their excellent 2009 article "Data Diagnostics Using Second-Order Tests of Benford's Law" in *Auditing: A Journal of Theory and Practice.*
3. Randomly generated data is also sometimes called "synthetic" data.

PART II

Statistical Approaches to Benford's Law

5

Goodness of Fit Scores

Most people use Benford's Law visually. That's what we did in the first four chapters: plotted data in a graph to observe whether it matched Benford's Law. The conclusions weren't analytical; they were matters of our own subjective professional judgment. Now we'll introduce a way to score our data. The score will tell us how well our data fits Benford's Law. Naturally, we call these *goodness-of-fit* scores. There are several advantages.

- First, it's fast. Manually creating and reviewing graphs takes a lot of time. Calculating a score can be done automatically with software. We can evaluate thousands of datasets in seconds.
- Second, scoring is quantitative. The visual inspection is qualitative. With visual inspection, we can't easily say how well a population fits Benford's Law, or compare whether some comply better than others. A score provides a simple, numerical comparison.
- Third, scoring allows us to say that our data does (or doesn't) follow Benford's Law. We do this by choosing a threshold (statisticians call it a *critical value*). If our score is above the threshold, we conclude that the data doesn't follow Benford's Law. There's no ambiguity.
- Finally, auditors should consider whether they have sufficient data for their analysis. Visual analysis is driven by professional judgment; there is no formula for determining how much data is needed. Quantitative methods have clear criteria for the number of records needed.

One important note about these scores: they are never 100% accurate. An old joke says that the answer to every statistics question is "maybe." Statisticians calibrate thresholds ("critical values") for scores through a risk assessment process. The most critical risk is a *false positive:* reporting

DOI: 10.1201/9781003562238-7

a problem when there isn't one. Although we can choose any risk level we wish, the most common is 5%. This means, if our data is above the threshold, there is only a 5% chance that it's due to random chance.

Auditors often think of data as facts. For example, if a purchasing card has a $500 limit, and there's a transaction for $600, it's an exception – period. There's no ambiguity, no randomness. Statistical tests work differently. From a statistical point of view, every data point is treated as a product of chance. Every conclusion is therefore subject to randomness. From a statistics or analytics perspective, concluding that there is fraud or error isn't possible. We can only say how likely it is – and whether it's within our risk tolerance or not.

Imagine you have a population of 1,000 purchasing card transactions. A statistician thinks of this like 1,000 rolls of a die. The numbers are facts, but they're shaped by many minute, random influences: random angles, heights, tiny variations in air pressure and wind, as well as random chance (noise). When we use statistics to reach a conclusion, we're not just reading facts. We are reading patterns influenced by randomness. That means there's always a chance the conclusion is wrong—not because the data is incorrect, but because of the inherent randomness of the universe.

5.1 The D-("Distance") Score

There are numerous scores you could use. They all have their own advantages and disadvantages. I recommend the D score, which was created by Cho and Gaines[1] to study campaign finance compliance. "D" stands for "distance." The D score provides a single score for the data being tested. This is a significant advantage over the Z score, which provides a score for each digit.

The D-score is relatively powerful, meaning that it doesn't require a lot of data to reach a reliable conclusion. The D-score works best with about 80 or more records. The critical values (thresholds) and their risk of false positives are: 10% chance of false positive at 1.21, 5% chance of false positive at 1.33, and 1% chance of false positive at 1.57.

The downside to the D score is that it isn't a standard function in Excel, Alteryx, SPSS, or other data analytics tools. You will need to calculate it yourself (in Excel) or create your own functions (in SPSS, Python, etc.).

The D score is defined as[2]:

$$D = \sqrt{\#\ of\ records} \times \sqrt{\sum_{d=1}^{9}(Frequency\ of\ d - Frequency\ expected\ by\ Benford's\ Law)^2}$$

where d is the digit.

A D score of 0 means that the dataset follows Benford's Law exactly. Higher scores indicate the data is farther away. The score is relatively okay with very small deviations, but provides larger penalties the bigger the difference is. For 95% significance, the critical value is 1.330. If you are using a critical value (threshold) any score larger than 1.330 should be suspicious.

A powerful facet of this score is that it responds to the size of your dataset. Imagine two datasets which match Benford's Law equally well. One dataset is 100 records, while the second is 1 million records. The larger dataset will have a worse score. Why? A small dataset could fluctuate a little based on random chance. A very large dataset should conform to Benford's Law almost exactly. The bigger the dataset, the pickier our test will be. The D-score formula presented above performs well when there are at least 80 records.

5.1.1 Example Calculation

Let's walk through an example of calculating a D-score. Table 5.1 shows the results of an ordinary Benford's Law analysis. The columns

Table 5.1 Benford's Law Results

DIGIT (d)	EXPECTED PROBABILITY	ACTUAL PROBABILITY
1	30.1%	25.98%
2	17.6%	18.48%
3	12.5%	14.49%
4	9.7%	10.72%
5	7.9%	8.25%
6	6.7%	7.36%
7	5.8%	5.57%
8	5.1%	5.14%
9	4.6%	4.02%

indicate the digit (d), the probability expected by Benford's Law, and the actual probability observed in the dataset. There are 7,512 records (not mentioned in the table). This data represents greenhouse gas emissions. For a visual analysis of this same data, see Chapter 4 (Figures 4.2 and 4.3).

For each digit, we start by subtracting the expected and actual probabilities. It doesn't matter what order you have the columns in: you could subtract the actual from expected and end up with the same result. Each one of those differences will be squared. Note that the squared values are always much smaller than the differences. You may need extra decimal places to accommodate them. Finally, sum up those squares. Table 5.2 demonstrates this calculation in detail. The result is a single number: 0.2374% (or 0.002374).

That's all the hard work. Let's plug these values into the D-score formula:

$$D = \sqrt{7{,}512} \times \sqrt{0.002374}$$

Continuing to solve the formula:

$$D = 86.67 \times 0.049 = 4.22$$

The D-score is 4.22. Since this is more than the critical value of 1.33, we conclude this data doesn't follow Benford's Law. Since we

Table 5.2 D-Score Calculations

DIGIT (d)	EXPECTED PROBABILITY	ACTUAL PROBABILITY	DIFFERENCE (EXPECTED – ACTUAL)	DIFFERENCE SQUARED
1	30.1%	25.98%	4.13%	0.1704%
2	17.6%	18.48%	−0.87%	0.0076%
3	12.5%	14.49%	−1.99%	0.0397%
4	9.7%	10.72%	−1.03%	0.0105%
5	7.9%	8.25%	−0.34%	0.0011%
6	6.7%	7.36%	−0.67%	0.0045%
7	5.8%	5.57%	0.23%	0.0005%
8	5.1%	5.14%	−0.02%	0.0000%
9	4.6%	4.02%	0.55%	0.0031%
			Total	0.2374%

used a critical value and accepted the 95% significance level, we also accepted a 5% chance of false positive. The auditors should keep in mind that there is a 5% chance this result is merely random chance. Since the dataset is fairly large (thousands of records), the D-score expects very close conformance.

5.2 MAD (Mean Absolute Deviation)

MAD is a score commonly used with Benford's Law both in research and the field.[3] Throughout the 1990s and early 2000s, it was recommended by the biggest names in Benford's Law. It's a fine score, but it has two disadvantages compared to the D score:

1. It does not factor in the population size. As a result, it doesn't perform well for small populations or small groups. Use it only for large datasets – the larger the better.
2. There are no known critical values. Subject-matter experts have proposed thresholds based on their experience. That's good, but not as robust as a mathematically derived critical value.

All that being said, there are also a couple of real advantages to the MAD score. It's much easier to calculate than the D score. Some statistical tools even have MAD built into their Benford's Law analyses. Finally, there is an intuitive meaning to MAD: it's the average "gap" between what Benford's Law expects and the actual data for each digit. That storytelling component can be persuasive in some situations.

The MAD formula is:

$$MAD = \frac{1}{9} \times \sum_{d=1}^{9} \left(\left| Frequency\ of\ d - Frequency\ expected\ by\ Benford's\ Law \right| \right)$$

The interpretation is the same as the D score. A score of 0 means the data matches Benford's Law perfectly. Bigger scores mean the data is less like Benford's Law. While the D score is (by design) very sensitive to big deviations in a single digit, the MAD score can be more forgiving.

Table 5.3 MAD Score Calculations

DIGIT (d)	EXPECTED PROBABILITY	ACTUAL PROBABILITY	DIFFERENCE (EXPECTED – ACTUAL)	ABSOLUTE VALUE
1	30.1%	25.98%	4.13%	4.13%
2	17.6%	18.48%	−0.87%	0.87%
3	12.5%	14.49%	−1.99%	1.99%
4	9.7%	10.72%	−1.03%	1.03%
5	7.9%	8.25%	−0.34%	0.34%
6	6.7%	7.36%	−0.67%	0.67%
7	5.8%	5.57%	0.23%	0.23%
8	5.1%	5.14%	−0.02%	0.02%
9	4.6%	4.02%	0.55%	0.55%
			Total	9.83%

5.2.1 Example Calculation

Let's use the same example to illustrate calculating the MAD score. Table 5.1 shows the Benford's Law results for a greenhouse gas emissions dataset. Table 5.3 illustrates the calculations. The first step of calculating the MAD score is only slightly different from the D-score. For each digit, we subtract the actual and expected probabilities. Just like the D-score, it doesn't matter which order the columns are in. We could subtract expected from actual and get the same results.

Next, we take the absolute value of each difference (effectively removing the negative signs). Finally, we sum up all those numbers. The result is 9.83% (or 0.0983).

Returning to the MAD formula:

$$MAD = \frac{1}{9} \times 0.0983 = 0.01$$

Unlike the D-score (as well as the chi-squared, Kolmogorov-Smirnov, and other scores), there are no known critical values for the MAD score. We don't have a statistical way to say that this value is too high or too low. The auditor either uses their professional judgment and experience or consults the work of a subject-matter expert to determine what an acceptable value is.

5.3 Honorable Mentions: Chi-Squared and Other Scores from the Math Department

The chi-squared test is one of the most commonly used scores in statistics. It's used in introductory statistics textbooks and first-year courses. It's the go-to score for tests using categorical data. That doesn't mean it's the best.

Chi-squared has some real advantages. It's available in almost every statistical tool. Its properties are well-known and highly researched. It has known critical values. It's also reasonably easy to calculate by hand if you need to. The major downside to the chi-squared test is that it is inefficient compared to D and other statistics. "Inefficient" means that it requires more data to work effectively. If you think of your statistical test as an engine, this one consumes more fuel (data) than other measures to reach the same conclusions.

Statistical texts also recommend other scores, such as the Kolmogorov-Smirnov (KS) and Kuiper scores. These are substantial improvements over chi-squared. You will see them used often in mathematical and statistical research, but rarely in accounting, auditing, information security, or other applied research. Since I don't recommend these scores, their formulas aren't provided here. They are commonly available in statistics textbooks and online.

5.4 Last Place: The Z Score

The Z score deserves a special mention as the worst choice. The results are overwhelmingly wrong, leading auditors to spend countless hours looking for issues that don't exist.

It operates differently than the rest of the scores presented here. Instead of providing one score for a dataset, it provides one score *per digit*. This allows the auditor or analyst to identify which digits are abnormal. This was popular in the 1990s and 2000s when computing technology was more limited and data analytics knowledge less common among practitioners. The idea was that you would identify which digit was abnormal than start reviewing transactions that start with that digit.

We have better tools today. This section describes existing challenges with the Z-score. If you are going to use it, this section also provides three improved approaches to reduce your false positives:

- Use another metric (such as the D-score or MAD) as a screening tool.
- Decide in advance which digits you are interested in.
- Only investigate digits which show a meaningfully large deviation from Benford's Law.

5.4.1 Challenges with the Z-Score

The Z-score comes with several challenges. First, it's computationally more difficult than all the other scores presented here. Suppose you are conducting a test of the first two digits. You only need a single MAD, D-score, etc. However, you need 89 different Z-scores! That's not just more calculation – it's a lot more to review. How could an auditor effectively review 89 different scores? Typically, practitioners look only at Z-scores above some threshold. The most common choices are to either review digits above the Z-scores critical value or to prioritize the largest deviations. Those are reasonable choices, but there can easily be a dozen or more digits that need to be reviewed.

Second, the Z-score has an immense false positive rate. Recall that statistical tests are calibrated with a "critical value": the chance of a false positive that we are prepared to accept. We can never have 100% certainty. Typically, scores are calibrated to accept a 5% chance of a false positive. That is, each test has a 5% chance of highlighting an error *even when there isn't one*. That 5% chance occurs for every test. For the D-score, MAD, and other tests, this isn't a problem because that one score covers the entire dataset. Statisticians call these "omnibus" tests for exactly that reason.

The Z score applies to only a single digit. When looking at the first digits of a dataset (which range from 1 to 9), we have 9 different scores. Each score has a 5% chance of being a false positive. That means the typical first-digit test has a **37%**[4] chance of a false positive! The problem is even worse for the two-digit test. There is a **99%** chance that the two-digit test highlights at least one false positive. On average, it will return 5 false positives every time it is used.

Unfortunately, commercial audit analytics tools often provide the Z score by default when running Benford's Law. This has probably been the single biggest factor in tarnishing the reputation of Benford's Law. These tools seemed to show deviations from Benford's Law all the time. After countless labor hours, auditors would decide there was really no problem and eventually give up on it entirely.

5.4.2 Improved Method 1: Combine the Z-score with an Omnibus Test

One of the best methods for reducing false positives is to combine the Z-score with one of the omnibus tests (like the D-score, MAD, etc.). This is the approach statisticians have used for almost a century in research and is commonly taught in research methods courses. It's easy and effective.

The procedure is two steps:

- *Test the entire dataset with an omnibus test (MAD, D, etc.).* This is the method previously described in the D-score and MAD sections. If the score is bigger than the acceptable threshold, then you conclude that the dataset warrants further investigation. If not, pass any further analysis.
- *Test individual z-scores.* If the dataset fails the D-score or MAD test, proceed to testing the Z-score. You have already concluded that the dataset is conspicuous. At this point, the only question is where the anomalies are. Calculate z-scores for each digit and look for unusual digits.

The first step weeds out many of the false positives that the z-scores would normally produce. You won't even look at z-scores unless your omnibus statistic (like D, MAD, etc.) indicates an anomaly. It's still possible for an individual z-score to be a false positive. In this case, you will have real anomalies alongside false positives. Nothing is perfect, but you've greatly increased your efficiency and effectiveness.

5.4.3 Improved Method 2: Know What to Look For

The second recommendation is not to test every digit with a z-score. Many people use Benford's Law as a high-level analytic without any particular fraud scheme or kind of error in mind. That's okay. You will be more effective if you can ground your analysis in a particular issue you want to detect. Auditors who target specific kinds of fraud or error are more likely to find something than those who walk in theoretically. Consider this example:

An auditor examining bank deposits. They could create z-scores for all 9 digits and follow up on values greater than 1.96 (the critical value for a 5% false positive rate). They will have a 5% chance of a false positive on each test. As mentioned earlier, this adds up to about a 37% chance of having at least one false positive.

A second auditor is conducting exactly the same analysis. They know that the Bank Secrecy Act requires deposits of $10,000 or more to be reported to the federal government. Someone evading this control would deposit an amount less than $10,000. A suspicious pattern would be the number "9" being too common and "1" being too infrequent. The auditor only looks at those two digits. Instead of a 37% chance of a false positive, they have about a 9.8% chance. Additionally, any red flags are more likely to be actionable because their test is tied directly to the kinds of errors they are interested in auditing. That's a tremendous gain!

5.4.4 Improved Method 3: Consider Impact of the Deviation

We consider a digit to be anomalous when the z-score is past our threshold (critical value). To be slightly more technical, the test is telling us that our data doesn't match Benford's Law and that the difference is big enough that it likely isn't random chance. This tells us that our results are likely *significant* (not a product of chance). It doesn't tell us they are important.

One way to improve our usage of the Z-score is to only look at digits which show a meaningful deviation from Benford's Law. This is similar to the concept of materiality: it may be different, but is it different enough to be practically important?. This approach is a two-step process:

- *Identify significant Z-scores.* For each digit, calculate the Z-score. If the Z-score is lower than our threshold, ignore it. If the Z-score is bigger than the threshold, continue the analysis.
- *Identify variances that are practically significant.* For each digit with a large Z-score, subtract the expected frequency (from Benford's Law) from the actual frequency in your dataset.

Give yourself a threshold (such as 1% or 0.01). If the difference is bigger than 0.01, investigate why. If it's less than 0.01, conclude that it's immaterial and move on.

The difference between Benford's Law and the actual frequency of that digit could be called "magnitude," "distance," or something similar. There's no analytical research suggesting what an appropriate rate is. Choose based on your specific context and risk tolerance.

Table 5.4 shows an example of this two-step analysis. Let's say we're using a Z-score threshold of 1.96 and a magnitude threshold of 1%. Digits 2 through 9 all have Z-scores within the acceptable range, so

Table 5.4 Two-Step Analysis Using Magnitude

DIGIT	NUMBER OF RECORDS	BENFORD'S LAW (EXPECTED FREQUENCY)	REAL DATA (ACTUAL FREQUENCY)	MAGNITUDE OF DIFFERENCE	Z-SCORE	CONCLUSION
1	1,951	0.3010	0.2598	0.0413	4.1579	Z >= 1.96. Anomaly detected. Magnitude of difference is about 3.9% – large enough to be meaningful. Review these transactions.
2	1,388	0.1761	0.1848	0.0087	0.8355	Z-Score < 1.96. No anomaly.
3	1,088	0.1249	0.1449	0.0199	1.8665	Z-Score < 1.96. No anomaly.
4	805	0.0969	0.1072	0.0103	0.9416	Z-Score < 1.96. No anomaly.
5	620	0.0792	0.0825	0.0034	0.3044	Z-Score < 1.96. No anomaly.
6	553	0.0669	0.0736	0.0067	0.6014	Z-Score < 1.96. No anomaly.
7	418	0.0580	0.0557	0.0023	0.2087	Z-Score < 1.96. No anomaly.
8	386	0.0512	0.0514	0.0002	0.0212	Z-Score < 1.96. No anomaly.
9	302	0.0458	0.0402	0.0055	0.4909	Z-Score < 1.96. No anomaly.

there's no need to look at them further. But the digit 1 has a Z-score above the cutoff, which means the difference from Benford's Law probably isn't due to random chance. Before jumping into an investigation, we check whether the difference is big enough to matter. Benford's Law expects 30.1% of values to start with the digit 1, but in our dataset, only 26.0% do. That's a difference of 4.1% – well above our 1% threshold – so we decide this is worth looking into.

Notes

1. This score was created by Wendy Cho and Brian Gaines, both in the Department of Political Science at the University of Illinois at Urbana-Champaign. See their article on campaign finance compliance titled "Breaking the (Benford's) Law: Statistical Fraud Detection in Campaign Finance" in *American Statistician* vol 61(3).
2. This formula is slightly modified from the original D score created by Cho and Gaines. It was modified by James Morrow at the University of Wisconsin-Madison in an unpublished paper called "Benford's Law, Families of Distributions, and a Test Basis." Morrow added the population size as a variable, which allows us to create critical values (thresholds).
3. Mark Nigrini popularized both Benford's Law and MAD as a metric for testing against it. See any of his numerous articles, publications, presentations, or other materials for countless examples. In particular, I recommend his book, *Forensic Analytics: Methods and Techniques for Modern Forensic Accounting Investigations.*
4. This can be calculated as a binomial probability. There are 9 trials, and each trial has a 5% chance of success.

6
Benford-Like Distributions[1]

Not all data matches Benford's Law. We've already seen many examples of spikes and other deviations that indicate problems. There are also deviations that are perfectly fine. Sometimes real data follows a curve that is similar to Benford's Law, but not exact. That's okay. Benford's Law is malleable. We can mold it into slightly different shapes.

Figure 6.1 shows several of these *Benford-like* distributions. There are some key characteristics they all share:

1. The first digit is the most common.
2. Every digit has a probability. They never hit 0%, although they might come close.
3. Each digit is less likely than the one before it. The fancy math word is "monotonically decreasing."
4. The probabilities form some kind of curve.

If your data doesn't have these traits, the examples in Chapter 3 can help diagnose why. The most common reasons are that the data has a clear minimum or maximum, or they come bundled in a narrow range. The techniques presented in Chapter 4 (such as the second-order test or data transformation) can help address some of these challenges.

This chapter requires some comfort working with mathematical formulas. Existing tools on the market do not have a way to leverage Benford-like distributions, so you will need to implement your own. This can be done in Excel and common programming languages.

DOI: 10.1201/9781003562238-8

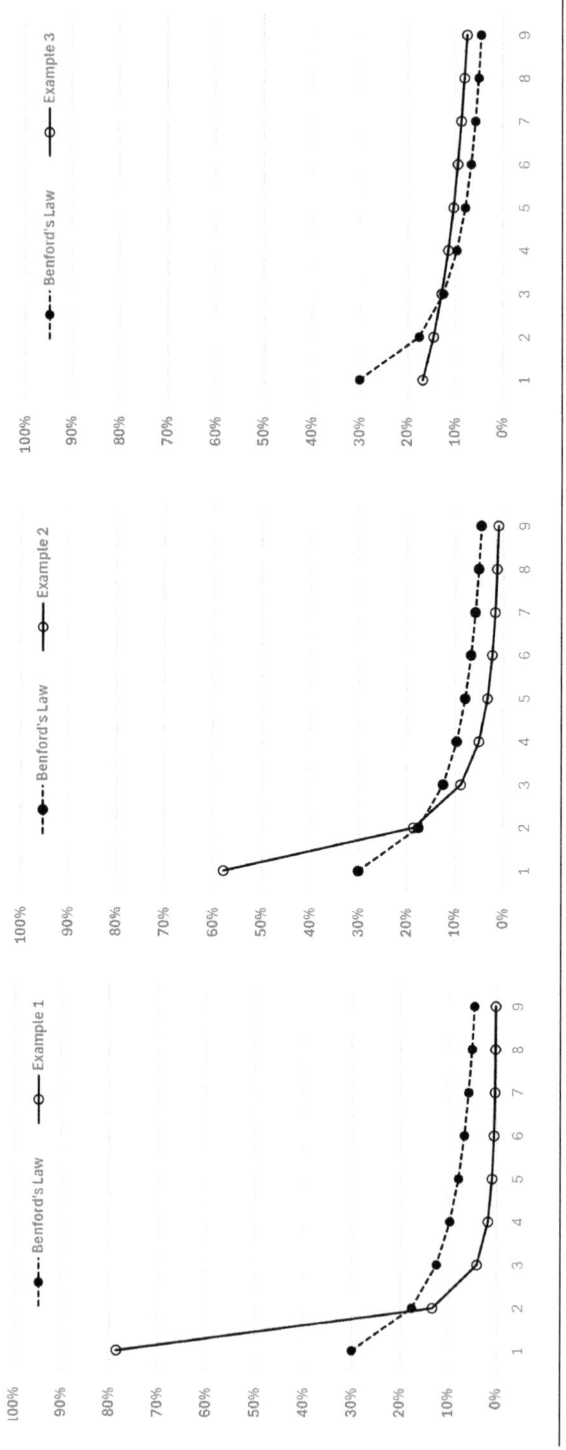

Figure 6.1 Examples of several Benford-like distributions.

6.1 The Generalized Benford's Law

We can slightly bend the curve of Benford's Law. To do that, we need to introduce some new variables into the formula. Let's call them p and q:

$$Probability\ (D) = log\left(1 + \frac{1}{P + D^{Q}}\right) * N$$

P and *Q* are discussed in more detail below. *N* is a normalization factor. You need all your probabilities to add up to 100%. *N* is a reminder to do that. For example, suppose you set $P = 5$ and $Q = 0$. The results would be Table 6.1. To make them equal 100% just divide each initial probability by the total.

The "Initial Calculation" column is the expected probability where $P = 5$ and $Q = 0$. We would expect that all the probabilities add up to 1 (or 100%). They don't! The solution is to take each number and divide it by the total (0.3979). The calculation for this first row is: 0.0669/0.3979 = 0.1682. The expected probability of a record starting with "1" in this adjusted formula is 16.82%.

6.1.1 What Are P and Q?

P and *Q* are new variables, or parameters, which expand the range of possibilities we can cover. *P* controls how curved the line is.

Table 6.1 Example of Calculating Probabilities for the Generalized Benford's Law

DIGIT	INITIAL CALCULATION	INITIAL VALUE/TOTAL
1	0.0669	0.1682
2	0.0580	0.1457
3	0.0512	0.1285
4	0.0458	0.1150
5	0.0414	0.1040
6	0.0378	0.0950
7	0.0348	0.0874
8	0.0322	0.0809
9	0.0300	0.0753
Total:	0.3979	1.0000

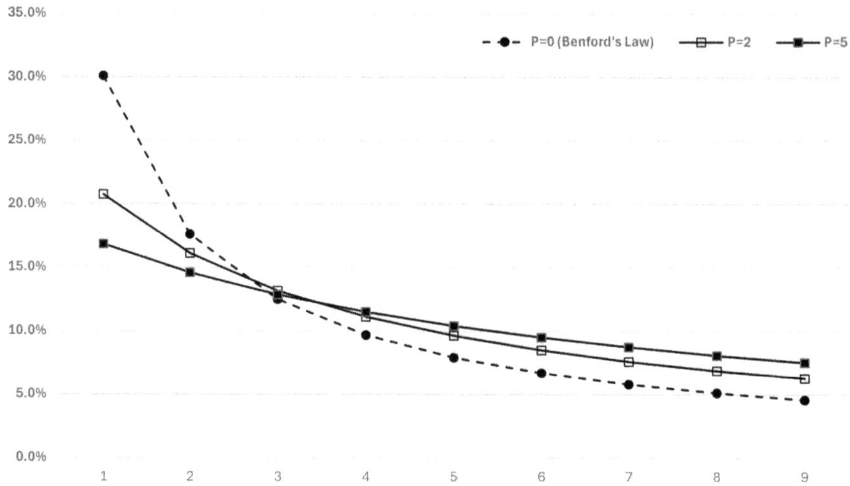

Figure 6.2 Effect of adjusting *P*.

As *P* increases, Benford's Law becomes less of a curve and more like a line. *Q* is the "peakedness" of the curve. Bigger values of *Q* will put a larger amount at the beginning and make the curve fall much more quickly. Statisticians call this "kurtosis." Figures 6.2 and 6.3 visualize the effects of adjusting *P* and *Q*.

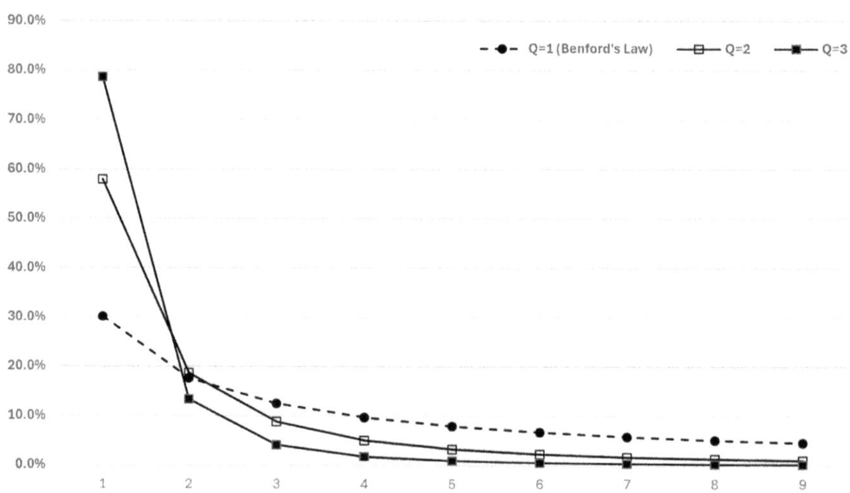

Figure 6.3 Effect of adjusting *Q*.

6.1.2 Is This Really the Same as Benford's Law?

Yes! Well, kind of. We created a new formula that covers many possible curves. The Benford's Law most practitioners know is just one possible curve. Now you have the power to construct equally valid curves to cover a variety of situations.

There's an easy way to reconcile this to the original Benford's Law. Set $P = 0$ and $Q = 1$:

$$Probability\ (D) = log\left(1 + \frac{1}{0 + D^1}\right) * N$$

That's the same thing as the original Benford's Law formula:

$$Probability\ (D) = log\left(1 + \frac{1}{D}\right).$$

6.1.3 Why Use These Benford-like Distributions?

If you are only looking at a single dataset (perhaps a single population at a high level) then it doesn't add much value. When only dealing with a single set of data, you can visually review the results and determine that your data has a slightly different shape. Easy.

There are many cases where this manual review is uneconomical. For example, if you are conducting an independent Benford's Law analysis for 1,000s of vendors, then you won't have the time to visually inspect all of those results. If the ordinary shape of your data isn't quite Benford's Law, then you could be getting hundreds of false positives. Adjusting Benford's Law to something more reasonable for your use case allows you to reduce false positives caused by the shape of your data.

There are also many cases where you shouldn't use a Benford-like distribution. If you are only reviewing a single population (or a small number of groups), then it probably isn't worthwhile to spend time adjusting parameters for a Benford-like distribution. You should also only use these distributions if you are confident that your observed deviation from Benford's Law isn't a result of fraud, waste, abuse, or some other interesting property. Finally, auditors should only use this technique if they are confident in their abilities to implement it. Both the IIA's standards (the International Professional Practices Framework) and GAO's standards (Governmental Auditing Standards) include a notion of competence. Using advanced techniques without understanding them is not only inadvisable, it is unethical.

6.1.4 Techniques for Picking P and Q

One of the most challenging aspects of this technique is picking suitable values of P and Q. There are essentially three approaches:

- Select values manually
- Use non-linear programming to determine the best value
- Write a script or program that iterates through many possible values and pick the best

Manually selecting values is the most straight-forward approach. Auditors could try several values of P and Q and experiment until they find values that work reasonably well for this data. They will not be the best (or optimized) values, but they could be marked improvements over the default Benford's Law. Doing this is relatively time consuming, which is why only a few values can be tested.

Nonlinear programming (NLP) is the most effective way to pick P and Q. NLP is a technique common in operations research, industrial engineering, and related fields. The analyst creates a formula which shows how P and Q are related to the overall fit to Benford's Law. Then it's relatively straight-forward to solve for the optimal values of P and Q – the values that fit your data the best. This is not easy. It requires advanced mathematical skills that are uncommon in audit analytics. Mistakes are easy to make and difficult to detect, so this approach is generally not recommended unless you have a subject-matter expert available.

Parameter sweeping is the middle group. It's the most economical solution, which gives good (but not optimal) values of P and Q. It's also much more accessible than NLP. Parameter sweeping means that a program will test a large list of possible values. For example, you could test 20 values of P and 20 values of Q: 400 potential combinations.

The script would return the goodness-of-fit score for each test. All the auditor needs to do is pick the best value.

Here's a simple example in pseudo-code:

```
List of Ps: [-2.0, -1.5, -1.0, -0.5, 0, 0.5, 1.0,
1.5, 2.0]
List of Qs: [0, 0.1, 0.2, 0.3, 0.4, 0.5, 0.6, 0.7,
0.8, 0.9, 1.0]

For each P in List of Ps:
      For each Q in List of Qs:
            Calculate Benford's Law probabilities
            using P and Q
            Compare actual data to Benford's Law
            probabilities
            Calculate goodness-of-fit score
            Output P, Q, and goodness-of-fit score.
```

6.1.5 Potential Values of P and Q

P and *Q* could be any real number. That's a big area to search through. For NLP that isn't an issue, but if you are manually experimenting or iterating through a script it will be beneficial to limit your search area.

P is the easier parameter. The default value is 0. Do you want to increase *P* (making Benford's Law more like a line) or decrease *P* (making it curvier)? Every data set will have its own needs, but ±10 is usually a very generous range. You could start by testing values closer to home (maybe ±3), expanding the range if necessary. If you find that your ideal value is between two numbers (maybe between 2 and 3), you can start targeting values in the middle (2.1, 2.2, 2.3, etc.).

Q is slightly harder. *Q* is used as an exponent. The default value is 1, but there are three ranges of values that will give different behavior:

- Increasing *Q* above 1 increases the peaks in the curve. More data will be expected to start with 1, and the curve will descend more quickly.
- Decreasing *Q* between 0 and 1 will decrease the peaks in the curve. Less data will be expected to start with 1, and the curve will descend more slowly.

- Decreasing Q to be negative flips the pattern: the majority of data will be expected to start with 9.

Negative Q values are expected to be uncommon. In the majority of cases, the most likely value of P is slightly smaller than 0, and the most likely value of Q is between 0 and 1.

6.2 Example Application – Inventory Adjustments

Consider an audit of inventory adjustments. The auditor requests their population and uses Benford's Law to evaluate the first digit of the *quantity* of each adjustment. For example, if an adjustment adds 10 units for a total cost of $3,000, the first digit is 1, not 3. The results are shown in Figure 6.4. The D-score is 1.33.

Clearly, the results do not match Benford's Law. The auditor could conclude that Benford's Law isn't applicable and use a different technique. They could conclude that there is an anomaly here and spend hours investigating. However, this is also a good opportunity to tune Benford's Law to look more like the data.

Is this a good idea? If the auditor is only reviewing the population once, then they could probably just stop here. However, if the auditor is going to compare many subsets (maybe running Benford's Law once

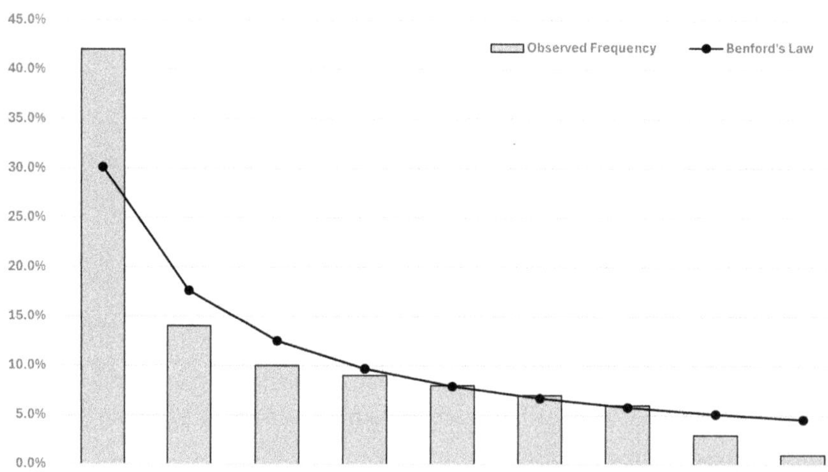

Figure 6.4 Benford's Law and inventory adjustment quantities.

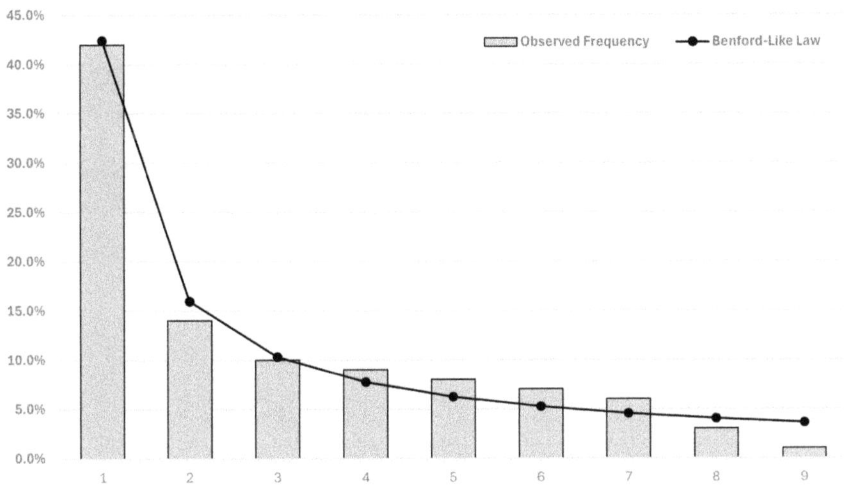

Figure 6.5 Benford-like Law and inventory adjustment quantities.

per inventory location), they will want to reduce false positives caused by this shape. The auditor can also observe that the key properties of a Benford-like distribution are observed here: 1 is the most common digit, all digits have data, etc.

The auditor manually experiments with several values of P and Q. They find that $P = -0.8$ and $Q = 0.88$ give good results. Their new results are shown in Figure 6.5. They could have used parameter sweeping or some automated technique to find better parameters. They used manual tests to locate P and Q because they recognized that their programming and technical skills may not be well-developed for this task. In this case, manual work suited their ethical standards, even though it may have been less efficient.

The curve is much improved visually. The new D-score is 0.05. That's a big decrease from 1.33! The new curve isn't perfect. The auditor could use a computer script to test hundreds of options and optimize the parameters more, but they conclude this is good enough for their task and move on.

The auditor could now put this into production as a continuous monitoring solution. The old curve would likely have resulted in hundreds of false positives each time the solution runs. This new curve fits the data much better, and the number of false positives is greatly reduced.

Note

1. Credit for this technique belongs to Dongdong Fu and Y.Q. Shi at the New Jersey Institute of Technology, as well as Wei Fang Su at the Huazhong University of Science and Technology. See their article "A generalized Benford's Law for JPEG coefficients and its application in image forensics" in the *Proceedings of SPIE – The International Society for Optical Engineering*.

7
Finding High-Risk Groups

Benford's Law can be used to find high-risk groups within your data. This could include finding a high-risk vendor within accounts payable data, finding high-risk servers within network traffic data, etc. In each case, the fundamental process is to determine which category field you are interested in (such as vendors) and calculate a goodness-of-fit score for each category (that is, for each vendor).

Several potential use cases exist:

- First, auditors might use this technique to select samples. For example, consider an accounts payable audit where the auditors are examining vendor setup and change controls. They could use this technique to select vendors with the highest scores for their sample selection. This technique can only be used to select categories (like vendors) that have many records each.
- Second, this technique could be used in audit planning to identify risks for each category. In the same accounts payable audit, the audit team could consider focusing their attention on individual vendors. Perhaps they want to review a small number of vendors in depth. They could use this technique to assess the relative risk of each vendor during planning.
- Third, this can be used to understand general trends or patterns in the data. The auditors could calculate their goodness-of-fit score for each vendor, then look at the results to reach a more general conclusion. For example, perhaps the vendors with the worst scores are all from the same region, were created by the same AP staff, etc. The audit team now has additional insight into their risks.

DOI: 10.1201/9781003562238-9

7.1 Approach to Identifying High-Risk Groups

This technique is a simple extension of the scores presented in Chapter 6. If you can calculate a score for a dataset, then you can also calculate a score for every group within that dataset. The first question will have to be, "what are my groups?". Your groups could be vendors, customers, employees, servers, cities, account codes, or nearly any other way of grouping your data. There are no special characteristics to consider. You want to select categories that are meaningful to your audit.

Remember that test statistics require a certain amount of data to be useful. As you work, it's helpful to include the number of records in each group. You will want to exclude groups that don't have enough data. My favorite is the D-Score, which performs best with at least 80 records. With less than 80 records, your results will be "noisy": you will have more false positives and charts with erratic ups and downs.

Second, consider what tools you have at your disposal. You could be calculating scores for hundreds of groups. Unfortunately, common audit tools have not kept pace with developments in Benford's Law, so we have to build our own tools. It is possible to do this in Excel. It's much easier using Python, R, or another general-purpose programming language.

If you are using Excel: create a new column in your data which contains the first-significant digit of each record. This is mostly accomplished with the LEFT() function, though you will need logic to account for negative numbers, currency symbols, etc. A pivot table can quickly calculate the frequency of each digit for each group. You will need to create a formula to calculate your test score. An example is provided in the next section.

7.2 Example Application: FinCEN Files

The Financial Crimes Enforcement Network (FinCEN) is a part of the US Department of Treasury that prosecutes financial crimes like money laundering. Financial institutions are required to report cash transactions of $10,000 or more to FinCEN. In 2020, trillions of dollars in reported transactions were leaked to an international group of

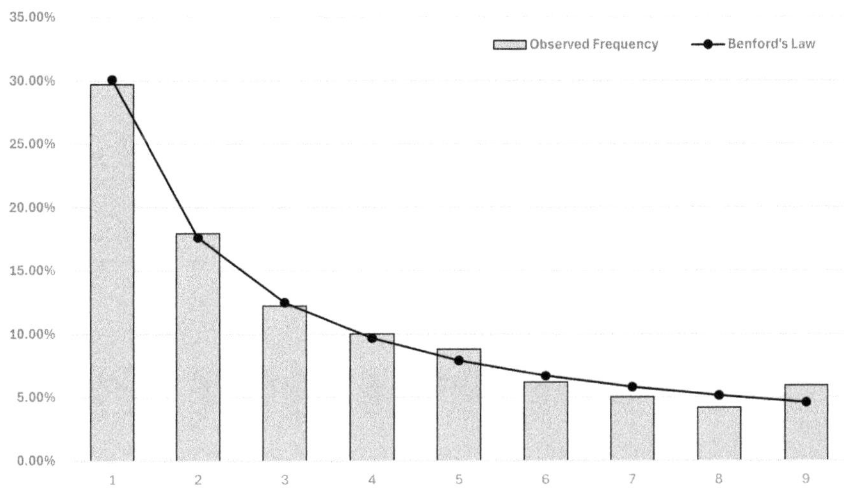

Figure 7.1 FinCEN reported transactions data compared to Benford's Law.

journalists.[1] That's a lot of data. How can the auditors narrow down their search to the most interesting transactions?

The data identifies both the sending and receiving financial institutions of each transaction. Although many institutions don't have enough transactions to justify using Benford's Law, they can further group these into countries. In this example, the auditors will look for countries with suspicious patterns of receiving funds. This could indicate they are part of money laundering schemes or other crimes.

First, let's visually inspect the first-significant digits of the entire dataset. Figure 7.1 visualizes the first-digit frequencies of the FINCEN transactions. The data shows a small spike around "9" and too few "1s," which could indicate someone avoiding the $10,000 reporting threshold. There are also too few transactions in the "6"–"8" range. This would be much more useful if they could isolate specific countries or institutions that are contributing to this problem.

Let's use the D-score to evaluate each receiving country individually. This analysis is easiest using an appropriate tool (like Python, R, or even Alteryx) if available. I'll present the work as an Excel document to help visualize what's going on.

Table 7.1 summarizes the first-digit frequencies for each country. First, create a new column in the data which includes the first digit for each amount. Next create a pivot table where each row represents

Table 7.1 Pivot Table Showing First-Digit Frequencies by Country of Receiving Financial Institution[a]

COUNTRY OF RECEIVING FINANCIAL INSTITUTION	FIRST DIGIT									
	1	2	3	4	5	6	7	8	9	D-SCORE
Australia	26.97%	19.10%	8.99%	14.61%	8.99%	5.62%	5.62%	3.37%	6.74%	0.72
Cayman Islands	19.05%	30.16%	14.29%	7.94%	6.35%	7.94%	4.76%	4.76%	4.76%	1.35
China	32.04%	20.44%	14.92%	11.60%	6.08%	4.97%	2.21%	4.42%	3.31%	0.88
Cyprus	33.15%	13.48%	14.04%	8.99%	8.43%	6.74%	5.06%	2.81%	7.30%	0.87
Estonia	31.97%	17.21%	12.30%	9.02%	10.66%	4.92%	4.92%	3.28%	5.74%	0.50
Germany	29.85%	16.42%	13.43%	11.94%	1.49%	8.96%	5.97%	8.96%	2.99%	0.69
Hong Kong	29.92%	16.67%	12.50%	10.23%	7.95%	6.06%	6.82%	4.92%	4.92%	0.27
India	38.10%	30.16%	3.17%	6.35%	4.76%	4.76%	6.35%	0.00%	6.35%	1.51
Latvia	32.06%	21.04%	10.42%	9.22%	9.02%	5.61%	3.61%	4.81%	4.21%	1.17
Netherlands	34.52%	17.26%	5.58%	11.68%	8.63%	6.09%	3.05%	7.11%	6.09%	1.30
Russia	33.74%	17.08%	12.35%	8.85%	9.05%	5.56%	4.53%	4.73%	4.12%	0.96
Singapore	25.63%	16.81%	14.71%	8.82%	10.50%	8.40%	4.20%	4.62%	6.30%	1.00
Switzerland	27.64%	17.75%	14.83%	10.11%	9.66%	7.42%	6.97%	2.25%	3.37%	1.08
Turkey	26.09%	17.39%	12.17%	13.04%	11.30%	5.22%	6.96%	3.48%	4.35%	0.72
Ukraine	30.77%	17.31%	9.62%	13.46%	5.77%	11.54%	5.77%	5.77%	0.00%	0.61
United Arab Emirates	**23.04%**	**17.83%**	**8.70%**	**6.52%**	**7.83%**	**3.48%**	**2.17%**	**4.78%**	**25.65%**	**3.53**
United Kingdom	37.50%	14.17%	10.00%	7.50%	9.17%	5.00%	9.17%	4.17%	3.33%	1.07
United States	28.84%	17.60%	14.61%	10.86%	8.24%	6.37%	2.62%	4.12%	6.74%	0.79

[a] Only countries with at least 50 records are included in this table.

a receiving country, each column is a different digit (1–9), and the values are the percentage of that country's records that start with each digit. Since they are using a goodness-of-fit score, they need to pay attention to how many records there are for each country. In this example, the results have been filtered to countries with at least 50 records.

Although the recommended amount is 80 records (see Chapter 5), the auditors accepted more risk because the number of countries was so low. This is a strategic choice: they can review more countries, because they filtered fewer out. The downside is that they have increased the risk of a false positive (that is, some apparent issues might turn out to be random noise). This might cost more time in the end. Sometimes it's worthwhile to accept these trade-offs, but always do so after evaluating the risks and benefits.

Which countries are the most suspect? Look for unusually high D scores. The highest belongs to institutions in the United Arab Emirates (UAE). Their D-score is 3.35: nearly 2.5x the nearest D-score! That's a clear outlier. Recalling the cut-off scores in Chapter 6, a D-score above 1.330 is suspicious. The UAE data is far above that threshold.

Look at the UAE data in more detail. About 26% of their records start with 9! That's an astounding deviation from Benford's Law. It's consistent with the auditors' theory of fraud, which suggests people would want to avoid detection by ensuring that their transactions are less than $10,000.

The auditors have narrowed down the results far enough that they can easily look at the data. Many transactions appear just below the $10,000 reporting threshold. Of the 230 transactions received by UAE institutions, 53 are between $9,800 and $9,999. Nearly all of these 53 were sent from the same institution: Trust Merchant Bank in the Republic of the Congo.

Benford's Law detected an anomaly. The auditors looked closer and identified a definitive story here. A single institution in the Republic of the Congo is sending a large number of transactions to the United Arab Emirates floating just below the $10,000 reporting limit. That sounds like something an audit or compliance team would like to know. Depending on the needs of the audit, they could continue looking at the next countries in the list (India and the

Cayman Islands). The test statistic is like a risk indicator: the bigger the score, the more risk there is. They could evaluate as much risk as they want. Eventually, they will find results that are no longer interesting.

Note

1. Thank you to the International Consortium of Investigative Journalists for making this data available. Download it at http://www.icji.org.

8
Time Series Applications

The applications covered so far all have the same workflow: test a single population (or sub-population) for compliance with Benford's Law. This chapter introduces a new workflow: tracking compliance over time. A single value tracked over time is called a time series.

The time series has a few applications in auditing. First, auditors might track a single metric over time and become interested when it hits a certain value. This is a common approach for continuous monitoring: track a risk metric and notify the audit team when it's too low or too high. Alternatively, they might monitor for large swings in the metric instead of predefined thresholds. Second, auditors might review data over a long period to identify time periods to sample based on unusual trends.

There are fundamentally two different ways to approach this problem:

1. We can group our data into time periods. For each time period, compare it to Benford's Law and compute a score. This technique is often used for batch data and is called *binning*. Accounting data is naturally grouped into accounting periods, which is a common opportunity to apply this technique.
2. We can examine all records within a certain trailing time period. For example, every day look at data for the last 60 days, compare it to Benford's Law, and compute a score. This technique is more common for streaming data and is called *windowing*.

Often the actual score for any time period is mostly irrelevant. Instead, the goal is to track compliance over time, identify the normal pattern, and then find deviations from the norm. Typical approaches include observing the highest or lowest scores (depending on the

DOI: 10.1201/9781003562238-10

metric used), observing deviations from common trends, or selecting thresholds and acting when the score surpasses the threshold.

8.1 Binned Data

In many cases, we will have many transactions or observations occurring in each period. A period could be any duration. In a financial technology setting, there could be hundreds of thousands of transactions per minute. In a traditional corporate accounting environment, there could be that many per month or quarter. The duration doesn't matter, so long as it's trivial to categorize every transaction into the right period. It's also important that every period has enough transactions to use Benford's Law effectively.

Using Benford's Law in this case is fairly easy: calculate a score for each period. Plot those scores over time. We are looking for:

- Significant increases or decreases. If your data has an ordinary range, look for dramatic changes outside that normal range.
- Changes in pattern. If your scores are very steady, look for turbulence. If your scores have normal ups and downs, look for any changes to that pattern.
- Movement beyond a threshold. You can set an upper or lower limit, then look at cases that go above or below that threshold.

The last technique is particularly well-suited for continuous monitoring. Imagine getting a file of journal entries every month. The application could calculate a fit score for that month and automatically notify the audit team if it doesn't adequately conform to Benford's Law. This is a great example of exception-based auditing: the audit team was called into action by an observed anomaly in the organization's data.

If you use a threshold, how do you set it? If your metric has known critical values (see Chapter 5), you can use those. Consider it a starting point, not the optimal solution. You may find that your organization's data has lots of variance (potentially resulting in many false positives) or is incredibly consistent (potentially resulting in many false negatives). Build it. Monitor it. Adjust over time. The MAD score does not have known critical values. Various authors and presenters have distributed their own thresholds for what constitutes a risk or suspicious MAD score. These are always specific to a certain business context and professional judgment.

It's also okay not to use a threshold. You can watch the graph over time and look for changes. Suppose you are looking at a year's worth of transactions, neatly binned into months. If one month has the worst score, then you might consider it to be the highest risk. This approach supports a risk-based sample selection mentality even without the threshold.

8.2 Example Application – Journal Entries[1]

Accounting data naturally comes in bins, making it an excellent application of this technique. Consider a common financial auditing population: journal entries. Journal entries are easy to group into periods (months, quarters, etc.). Often, we want to identify a period that's higher risk so we can focus testing on that period.

The example below illustrates Benford's Law using 12 months of journal entry data. For each month, the first-significant digit of each journal entry line item was examined using Benford's Law. A MAD score was calculated for each month. Figure 8.1 shows 12-months of MAD scores for this journal entry population.

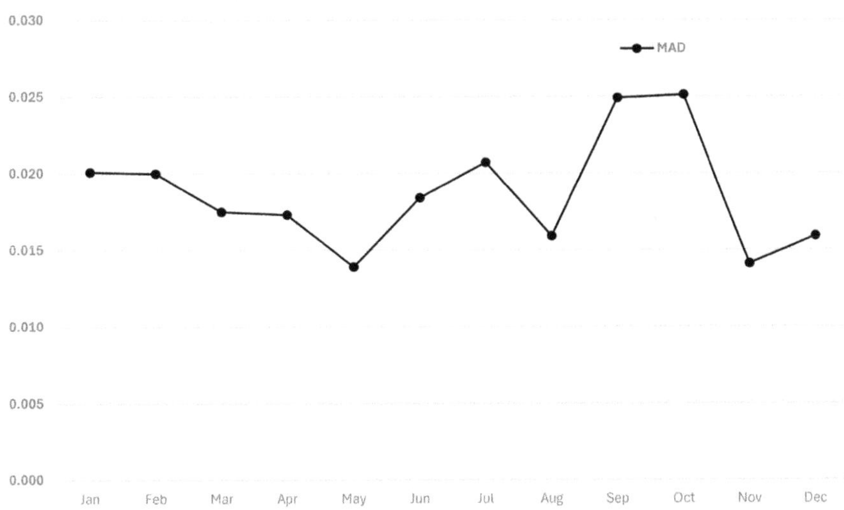

Figure 8.1 Monthly MAD scores for journal entries.

Note that the MAD score goes up and down throughout the year. There's no obvious minimum or maximum to use as a threshold. The trend has clear peaks and valleys. However, it isn't clear that the peaks line up with the end of the quarter exactly. A high score means weaker connection to Benford's Law. We could recommend that our audit team focus on September and October, the two months with the highest score.

Binning has a straight-forward application to many common audit procedures. For example, SOX testing typically involves sampling time periods and evaluating a control in the sampled period. A monthly control might involve selecting 2–4 months to review. This technique directs the auditors to periods where conformance to Benford's Law is the worst – or the most interesting.

How would the auditors select a month to review? The simplest approach is to look for periods with the worst conformance to Benford's Law. September and October both have high MAD scores, so they may be viable samples. A second approach is to look for large changes. September is the biggest jump in the MAD score. A third approach is to look for trends. January–May is a period of decreasing MAD scores (and therefore increasing conformance to Benford's Law). This pattern changes in June, so what changed?

Our ability to spot patterns would be much stronger if we had many years' data. For example, it could be that September and October typically have high MAD scores due to some repetitive intercompany journal entries (or some other kind of journal entries with similar amounts). The only way to spot this is to have several years' data and compare. Subject-matter knowledge is also valuable in this kind of analysis. An auditor who understands the normal timing and behavior of journal entries is more likely to identify unusual trends.

8.3 Windowed Data[2]

Sometimes our data won't be neatly contained in periods, or our periods won't have enough transactions to use Benford's Law well. This could be especially true with streaming data: data sources that report events in real time such as industrial sensors, transaction processing, cybersecurity monitoring, etc. For example, suppose we are analyzing events in a cybersecurity context. There could be hundreds of events recorded each minute – or none at all. We could bin our events into days (or hours), but that might be too vague to be useful and again, there might be no data present for some periods.

The solution is to construct a floating *window*[3] of data. For each transaction, look back at all the data in a certain amount of time and calculate your fit score. In our example, that could mean taking each security event in the log, identifying all events recorded in the prior 10 minutes, calculating our Benford's Law fit score, and plotting it over time.

One advantage is that this method doesn't assume a certain period (like months, days, etc.). Although in accounting and SOX applications, periods are easy to assume, in many other applications that would be undesirable. For example, a burst of suspicious events occurring in the span of a few minutes might be interesting in our cybersecurity example. It's also advantageous when suspicious behaviors cross periods: imagine a string of fraudulent transactions that occur partially in September and partially in October. An analysis which focuses on evaluating both months independently would be unlikely to capture the suspicious pattern. A final reason to consider windowing is when response time is critical. For example, waiting until the end of the week or the end of the month to detect a realized cybersecurity threat is often unacceptable. Windowing the data to focus on the most recent 10-minute interval could detect a threat in 10 minutes.

8.4 Example Application – Law Enforcement Gun Usage

The City of Phoenix, Arizona, reports interactions where police officers pointed a gun at a person ("PGP"). This data is reported daily and is available (at the time of writing) on the city's data portal. Their data is easily aggregated to count the *number* of such interactions each day. Although this isn't an example of fast-streaming data, we can use the windowing technique to identify a time period where the PGP data appears unusual.

First, we should identify how large our window is. Ideally, we could have hundreds of records in each window. Since our data is daily, it wouldn't be useful to aggregate hundreds of days. What would you do with a result that said a 100-day period was abnormal? As a starting place, let's consider a window of 50 days. That's less data than is ideal, so our scores might fluctuate more than normal due to random chance.

For each day, we use Benford's Law to examine the prior 50 days. For example:

- The June 30 value is the MAD score covering the dates May 11–June 30.
- The August 15 value is the MAD score covering the dates June 26–August 15.
- The December 1 value is the MAD score covering the dates October 12–December 1.

We are looking at the first digit of the number of PGP interactions on each day. So if there were 27 PGPs on a certain day, the first digit is "2." That also means for the first 49 days, there is no data to report, because 50 days haven't elapsed yet.

Figure 8.2 plots the values of the test statistic over time. I used the MAD score. As you can see, there is a clear trend: ups and downs over time. The normal trend is broken around February 2022. The largest value appears on February 9th, while a plateau occurs between April 10 and May 25, 2022.

What does the chart tell us? There is a normal trend, with regular ups and downs across time. Starting in January 2022, there is a sharp increase in the MAD score. Since a MAD score of 0 is ideal, this represents something an audit team may be interested in. This spike subsides, but April–June 2022 are another spike which plateaus. The first spike peaks on February 1, which tells us that in the 50-day period before February 1 (December 13, 2021–February 1, 2022), our data suddenly broke away from Benford's Law. The plateau later on tells us that mid-January to April are also likely interesting.

What could explain this increased MAD score in the December 13–February 1 period? The most obvious would be a change in police activity. That doesn't mean more or less gun-related activity, just a change. There could also be a change in incidents during that time period, which had an indirect effect of changing police behavior. A third possibility is a change in reporting practices. Auditors would need to delve into that period to understand why this change occurred. This technique was successful in highlighting *where* to look.

If your data is truly streaming, you can use this same technique, but omit the step where data was aggregated by day. You can simply use the time stamp on your events or transactions directly.

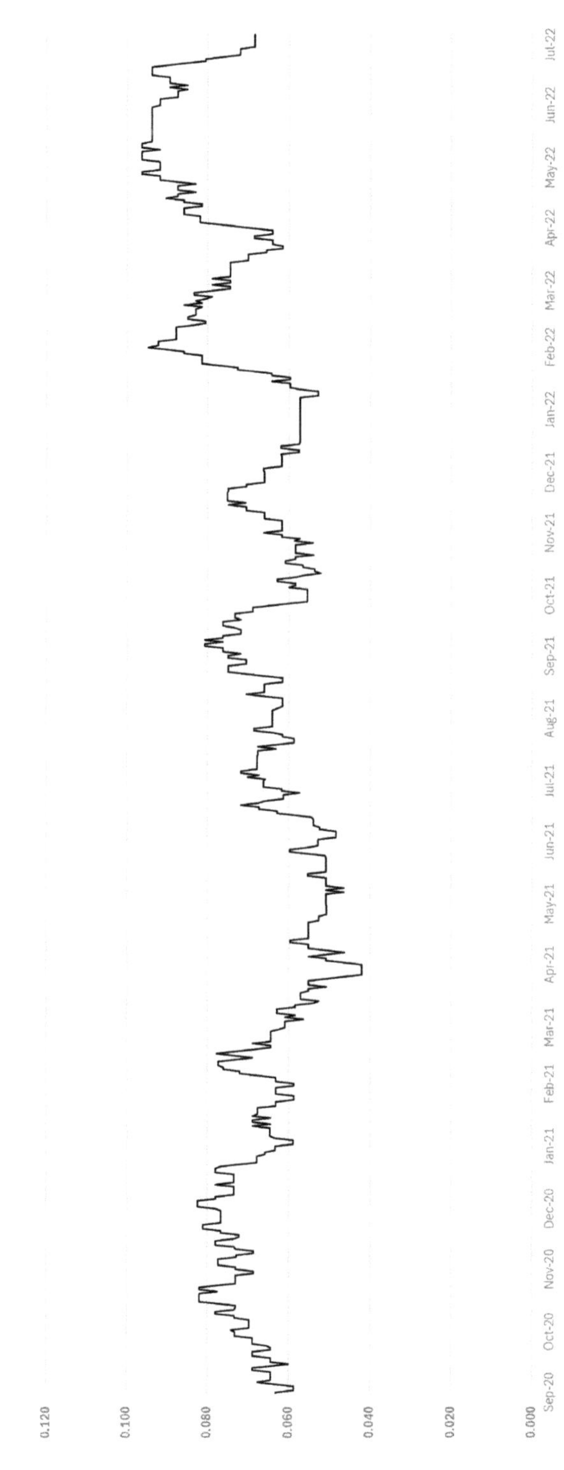

Figure 8.2 Mad scores for PGP interactions using a 50-day window.

Notes

1. J. Carlton Collins published this data in the *Journal of Accountancy* article titled "Data mining your general ledger with Excel."
2. This technique was developed by Malcolm Sambridge and H. Tkalčić at Australian National University, and A. Jackson at ETH Zurich. They innovated this technique for detecting earthquakes in seismograph data. See their work in *Geophysical Research Letters* (Volume 37, Issue 22) for the full details.
3. The term "window" comes from SQL where window functions are commonly used for this purpose.

9

Benford's Law and Machine Learning

Artificial intelligence (AI) and machine learning (ML) are popular topics in the world of audit analytics. While the world is currently engrossed in Generative AI, undoubtedly, the most commonly used approach to AI is ML. ML models read data and extract understanding from it. Using that understanding, they can make predictions such as forecasting future values or assigning observations to categories.

Benford's Law can be used alongside ML in many ways. This chapter explores several common approaches. At its core, Benford's Law is a diagnostic tool for data quality. The most obvious application is to use Benford's Law to screen the quality of data being fed to a ML model. Within a model, Benford's Law goodness-of-fit scores (such as the D-score or MAD) can be used either as a feature or response variable. Finally, Benford's Law could be used to evaluate the model itself.

This chapter does not provide a foundation in AI or ML. It is intended for audit analytics teams, data scientists, or others who already possess some understanding of these techniques. The goal is to provide a set of approaches for leveraging Benford's Law for these more advanced applications.

9.1 Data Quality Monitoring

ML models require input data. Benford's Law is a diagnostic tool for a variety of data quality problems. The simplest marriage is to use Benford's Law to identify data quality problems. This usage is really identical to all the other examples covered in this book: take some input data, use Benford's Law. If there are irregularities, then investigate.

Goodness-of-fit scores (such as D-score or MAD) are required for this approach. ML models can have hundreds of columns of input

DOI: 10.1201/9781003562238-11

data. It's impractical to visually review Benford's Law for every column. Instead, calculate a score and send a notification if a particularly high score is observed. Longitudinal (time series) techniques (covered in Chapter 8) can be used to monitor data quality over time. This allows you to monitor for model drift. Establish a baseline MAD score during model development or tuning, monitor the MAD score over time, and if the MAD score deteriorates or shows a jump or crash, intervene.

Although a tremendous technique for ML operations (ML Ops), this same approach can be used in any high-volume data management scenario. Consider an audit analytics team that receives a journal entry file every month. They could use historical data to determine what an ordinary MAD score looks like. Each month when they receive the file, they could observe the MAD score and see if it's similar to the baseline score. If it isn't, they might inspect the file to see if there is an emerging data quality problem. This can be used with teams of any size from a single-person audit analytics team up to an enterprise-wide CDO office with hundreds of employees.

There's always a substantive decision to make. Is my goodness-of-fit score decreasing because of data quality, or because someone has manipulated the data? Often auditors don't pay attention to data quality, and often data engineers don't consider the possibility of fraud or manipulation. The audit analyst has a hand in both disciplines and should consider whether their data quality framework potentially also detects items of auditable interest. Benford's Law does both.

9.2 Benford's Law as a Feature

Features are the columns of data used as inputs into a model. In a predictive model, features are used to predict an outcome variable. Benford's Law goodness-of-fit scores can be excellent features for the right kind of model. For example, models that predict risks, or categorize records based on some notion of risk, can often be improved by incorporating Benford's Law.

Predictive models can leverage this technique. For example, a payment processing team may have a dataset with known instances of fraud or error. The auditors could use a predictive model with Benford's Law as an input to help predict other instances of fraud. They include these sample selections in their audit, or they use these scores to estimate overall fraud risk in the payment processing function

Auditors usually do not have this kind of labelled data: we don't already know which records represent fraud or error. Instead, it's more common to use an unsupervised anomaly detection approach such as isolation forests. As an example, consider an audit of accounts receivable. Auditors are examining credit memos. They could use a ML algorithm to help detect unusual credit memos for sampling. To do so, they start by identifying a list of flags (the features) for the model. Common examples include:

- Is the credit memo on a weekend or holiday?
- Is the amount a clean, even amount (like $1,000)?
- The amount of the credit memo, perhaps expressed as a Z-score.
- Frequency of credit memos for this account.

The auditors might consider using Benford's Law as another feature. They would introduce a new feature representing the MAD score for all transactions related to a particular customer, AP staff, or account code. This new score would be fed into the model, which would consider it when determining what is (or isn't) an anomaly. Although this looks new, it's just a statistically more advanced example of the basic reasons for using Benford's Law: Benford's Law anticipates kinds of risks that other red flags don't. Benford's Law is another red flag, which can improve the overall performance of a model.

An example of this kind of scorecard is presented in Table 9.1. This represents the input of the anomaly detection algorithm. The output will be a score for each record (the vendor) representing how much of an anomaly that vendor is.

Table 9.1 Example Dataset Incorporating Benford's Law as a Feature

VENDOR	CREDIT MEMO NUMBER	WEEKEND OR HOLIDAY?	AMOUNT	# OF MEMOS FOR ACCOUNT	MAD SCORE FOR VENDOR'S TRANSACTIONS
Vendor A	CM-4821	0	$63.17	11	0.0215
Vendor B	CM-9375	1	$100.00	3	0.0074
Vendor C	CM-1603	0	$278.43	6	0.0132

Remember that calculating a goodness-of-fit score requires a certain number of records in each group. You can't calculate a score for a single record. That means you will have to decide how to group your data when constructing your scores. In some cases, it's clear from the problem what your group should be. Often you will want to experiment until you find the best features for your model.

9.3 Benford's Law as an Outcome Variable

Goodness-of-fit scores are usually used to describe how well a certain data set fits Benford's Law. An auditor might eventually ask deeper questions: *why* does the data fit (or not fit) Benford's Law? Does it fit better or worse in certain circumstances? What factors influence how well a certain vendor, entity, etc. will follow Benford's Law?

In these cases, a model could be built that uses the goodness-of-fit score as the outcome variable (also called a target or response variable). The model can analyze a variety of features with the goal of predicting the goodness-of-fit score for a certain entity. Let's use the same audit described in the previous section. The auditors are examining credit memos. They have calculated a Benford's Law score for each customer and are now trying to understand why some customers fit Benford's Law better than others. Figure 9.1 depicts their model:.

Notice that the features have changed. In the previous model, the auditors were looking for unusual credit memos. This model explains the MAD score for each customer. The features need to reflect properties of the customer, not individual credit memos. For example, the amount of the credit memo is no longer a feature (because we are dealing with the entire customer now, not individual credit memos). It has been replaced by aggregate statistics like the average credit memo size.

It might seem unusual to "predict" the MAD score when the auditors can easily calculate it from the credit memo data. Doing this has several benefits. First, it helps the auditors understand[1] what factors are driving high or low MAD scores. This is a kind of root cause analysis. For example, they may find this model works well, but the number of credit memos doesn't have much predictive value. That's learning something important: large (or small) numbers of credit

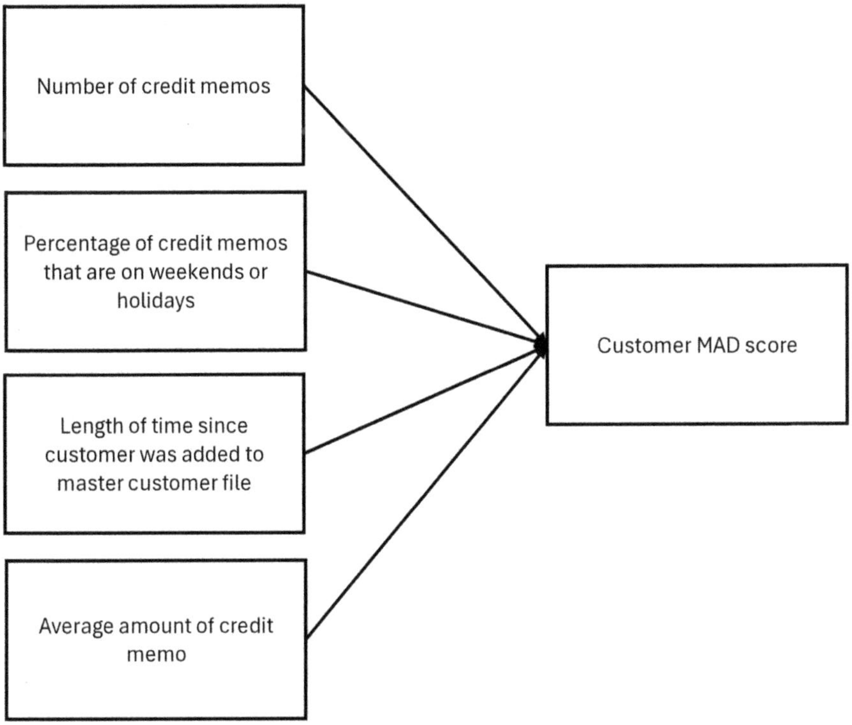

Figure 9.1 Predicting the MAD score for a customer.

memos aren't indicating any risks that Benford's Law is detecting. As they refine the model, they might also identify new factors that are important.

These insights can help improve future risk assessments. For example, the auditors might conclude that customers in certain countries are likely to have higher MAD scores. They might include this in future risk assessments, changing the way they target audit work and samples. The process of building the ML model helped them develop useful insight into part of their business.

Second, the model might be wrong in interesting ways. Suppose the model predicts that a certain customer should have a low MAD score (and therefore be relatively "safe"), but in reality, it's MAD score is high. We should ask why the model believes this customer is safe. We might learn something interesting. Similarly, what if the model predicts a customer is high-risk when its actual MAD score is low? Has the model intuited a risk we don't yet understand? Alternatively, maybe the customer is low-risk for some unusual reason and we can build that into the model.

One caveat about this predictive approach: predictive models fundamentally do not explain *why* something happens. Predictive models *predict* outcomes. They search for features (or combinations of features) that are correlated to the outcome. That makes them exceptionally valuable when we want to predict which groups are likely to follow Benford's Law, or what the overall conformance might be. Predictive models do not *explain* the outcomes. A robust explanation for why certain groups match Benford's Law should use inferential statistics, not predictive modelling. Nonetheless, predictive models can help us humans develop insights before submitting them to more robust testing.

9.4 Benford's Law for Evaluating ML/AI Models

Benford's Law can also be used to evaluate ML or AI models. Models produce a large number of internal values (often called weights or coefficients, depending on the kind of model). We can use Benford's Law to analyze those values and determine whether the model appears suspect.

This approach is often counterintuitive to people in the ML community. Often, the weights (or coefficients) themselves aren't very interesting. We are focused on the predictions, not the intermediate values produced within the mechanics of the algorithm. There are primarily two sets of research that establish the foundation of this approach:

1. The earliest research in Benford's Law was a hunt for different kinds of data that follow Benford's Law. Frank Benford's own research demonstrated that many kinds of physical values follow Benford's Law. Throughout the 1940s–1950s, several articles demonstrated that statistical tables follow Benford's Law. This is certainly before the time of modern data science, but it demonstrates a foundational reason to suggest the possibility.
2. Extant research appeared in the 2020s exploring the application of Benford's Law to neural network weights. The literature is currently small, but is growing. Benford's Law for regression tables had been established previously, which covers a large number of models using the general linear model.

Benford's Law can detect a variety of different features in data. In neural networks, the primary focus has been on evaluating accuracy for model validation.[2] Validation typically requires reserving data for the validation process. Benford's Law has been successful as a proxy for validation accuracy. That is, a low score using Benford's Law indicates a dataset will have validation accuracy. If validation accuracy measures are not available, an auditor (or other professional) could use Benford's Law on the model weights. Alternatively, a developer could use Benford's Law instead of a traditional validation process if they needed to conserve data.

Data scientists often have other methods for measuring accuracy or detecting model validation challenges. However, auditors may be responsible for audits of ML models. Audit interest in model governance and ML oversight grows every year. There are also specialized fields such as model risk audits in the insurance sector. In these circumstances, the audit team may want to critically evaluate the metrics provided by management. Benford's Law provides one mechanism to do this.

Notes

1. We should distinguish between *predictive analytics* and *diagnostic analytics*. This machine learning model has predictive value: it can identify features that are useful for predicting MAD scores. It does not identify or explain causal relationships. Nonetheless, exercises like this can help us develop insights into the way our business processes work.
2. See for example, the work of Sahu, Java, and Shaikh. Their article "Rethinking Neural Networks with Benford's Law" appears in the proceedings of the *Fourth Workshop on Machine Learning and the Physical Sciences*.

10
Beyond Base-10

We've only been concerned with ordinary base-10 (decimal) numbers so far. Our ordinary numbering system uses base-10, so it's highly unlikely that most auditors would ever need to consider a different scenario. However, there are applications in IT security where there is the possibility of encountering data in other bases, especially hexadecimal and octal. Fortunately, Benford's Law is easily expanded to cover any base.

10.1 The Benford's Law Formula for Different Bases

Chapter 2 introduced the basic formula for Benford's Law. It relies on a logarithm. Did you notice that "10" in the subscript? That defines the base of the logarithm. Changing Benford's Law to use a different base is as easy as changing that subscript. For example, the formula for Benford's Law in octal (base-8) is below.

$$Prob(D) = log_8\left(1 + \frac{1}{d}\right)$$

The resulting probabilities are in Table 10.1.

Note that the digits are now 1–7. The number of digits is always one less than the base. In our ordinary base-10 number system, there are 9

Table 10.1 Benford's Law in Octal (Base-8)

DIGIT	PROBABILITY
1	33.33%
2	19.50%
3	13.83%
4	10.73%
5	8.77%
6	7.41%
7	6.42%

Numbers do not add up to 100% due to rounding.

DOI: 10.1201/9781003562238-12

possible first-significant digits (1-9). In base 8, there are 7 (1–7). Zero may not be the first-significant digit in any base.

10.1.1 Special Note about Binary

This formula works exactly the same for binary (base-2) data. However, you'll never need to use it. Binary has two digits: 0 and 1. Remember when we use Benford's Law, we are examining the first-significant digit: the first non-zero digit. If we exclude 0, the first-significant digit in binary must always be 1. So although Benford's Law works with binary, the results are trivial.

10.2 The Concept of Base Invariance

Benford's Law can be used in any base. It also has a fairly unique property: base invariance. Base invariance means if a dataset conforms to Benford's Law in one base, then changing the data to a new base won't change that fact. Similarly, if a dataset doesn't conform to Benford's Law, then changing it to a new base won't somehow make it match Benford's Law.

We can leverage this property when data in a particular base is challenging. For example, supposing we had hexadecimal (base-16) data, we could safely transform it into decimal (base-10) without doing any harm to the analysis. There's no mathematical reason to prefer any particular base. We should pick the base that is most convenient for our analysis. This is base-10 in nearly all cases, but remember you have the option.

10.3 Example Application – Determining the Base of a Dataset

Auditors rarely examine numbers that aren't in base-10. However, a particularly colorful example comes from the real-life world of treasure hunting. The Beale Ciphers are a series of three encrypted messages published in 1885. One message was allegedly deciphered by the publisher. Solving the cipher required taking each number in the encrypted message and looking it up in the Declaration of Independence (for example, the number "10" means "look at the 10th word"). The decyphered text explained that the other two encrypted messages would contain the location of a treasure trove, as well as the rightful heirs to that treasure.

The remaining two ciphers have not yet been solved. Viktor Wase,[1] a researcher in Sweden, used Benford's Law to evaluate whether the three ciphers represent base-10 numbers. In short, they calculated a score representing how well each cipher fit a particular base. A low score means that the cipher probably represents numbers in that base.

His results are in Figure 10.1. As you can see, all three match base-10 quite well (their lines are low), but could be anywhere between base-8 and base-10. That's not particularly conclusive. However, Cipher 2 (the one allegedly solved by the publisher) is completely different! Why would the solved cipher be different from the two unsolved ones? If they are legitimate, there shouldn't be a difference. One interpretation is that the two unsolved ciphers were created in a different way than the solved one. For example, the solved cipher may have been deliberately constructed to refer to the Declaration of Independence, while the other two ciphers are arbitrary numbers.

Although novel, visually inspecting this chart is similar to the time-series charts discussed in Chapter 8. The key is to identify a pattern and then identify something different from the pattern. In this case, the pattern is that Ciphers 1 and 3 have a similar shape: they initially have a high value and sharply crash downward until around

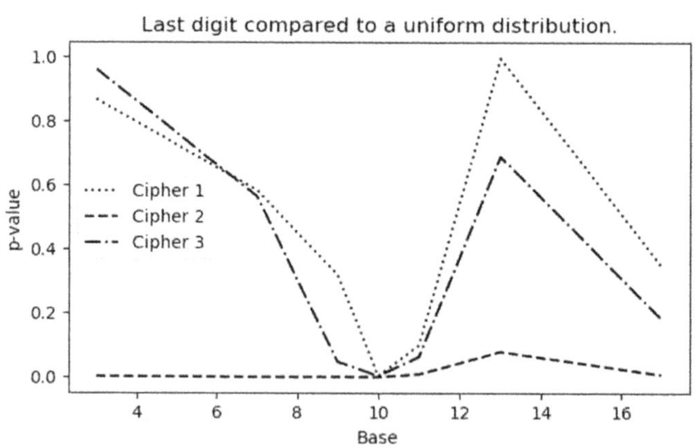

Figure 10.1 Last digit compared to a uniform distribution.

Note: Reproduced with permission of Viktor Wase. Originally published in *Proceedings of the 3rd International Conference on Historical Cryptography.*

base-7. They both remain low between base 7–10. Cipher 2 has an entirely different shape: scores are typically low, except at base 9. No matter what the particulars of the score are, it's clear that it has an entirely different pattern from the other two.

10.4 Example of Base Invariance

Base invariance is unlikely to be important in an audit scenario. This example is intended to help illustrate the concept. The Nebraska Department of Motor Vehicles collects motor vehicle taxes. Taxes are collected at the county level. In 2023, $331 million was collected in total from Nebraska's 93 counties.[2]

Figure 10.2 compares Benford's Law to the first digits of the total collected from each county. Visually, the data clearly doesn't follow Benford's Law. The D-statistic is 1.40, which is more than the critical value of 1.33 and confirms that the data doesn't follow Benford's Law. The data shows two humps: one on the digits 1 and 9, the second on the digits 4 and 5. A few potential interpretations could be:

- This pattern resembles revenue management in corporate financial statements. County officials could have psychological or social pressure to collect amounts that look smaller. For example, numbers like $100,000 may feel more comfortable than a

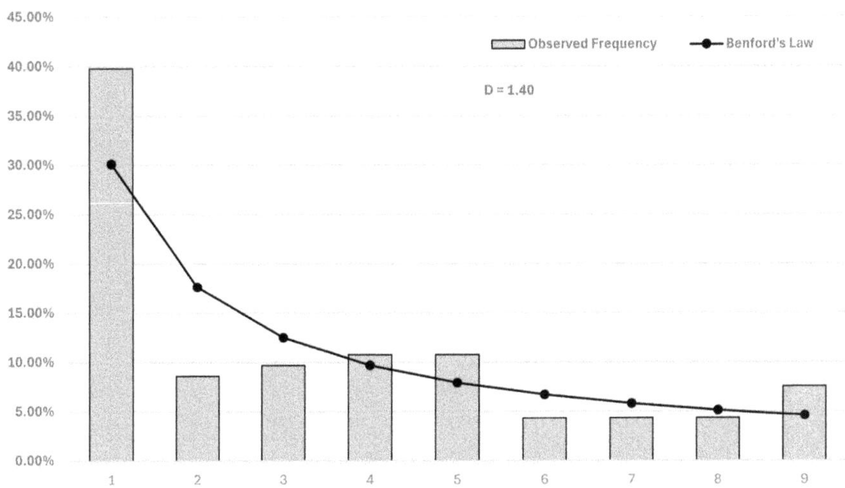

Figure 10.2 Nebraskan counties' motor vehicle tax collections compared to Benford's Law.

number like $110,000.[3] This seems doubtful, since county officials and staff don't set tax rates, nor can they meaningfully impact the number or kind of vehicles being registered.

- Motor vehicle taxes are based on the number and kind of vehicles being registered in that county. Perhaps this indicates something interesting about the number of vehicles in each county, or the kind of vehicle the people in that county are likely to drive.
- The number of records is relatively small (93). Although that should be enough to get good performance out of the D-score, random chance is still a possible interpretation.

How would this data look in different bases? To illustrate base invariance, let's examine the exact same data in octal (base-8) and hexadecimal (base-16). Excel's base() function can translate the data into the appropriate base. The only change needed to Benford's Law is to specify the correct base in the log() function.

Figure 10.3 shows the same data when converted to octal and hexadecimal. The data continues to perform poorly compared to Benford's Law. Both charts show spikes, though the meaning of those digits is challenging to understand. The D-scores have shifted. The D-score in base-10 was 1.33, but in base-8 it is 1.62 and in base-16

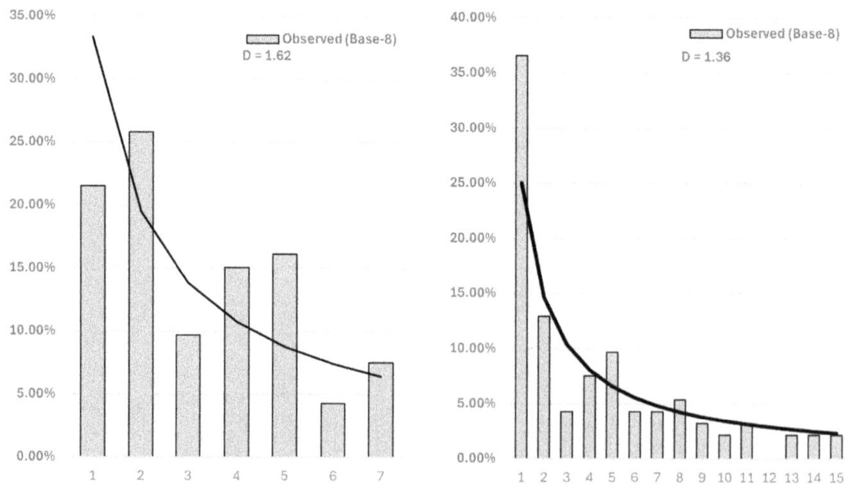

Figure 10.3 Nebraskan counties' motor vehicle tax collections in base-8 and base-16.

it is 1.36. While that is some shifting, the conclusion in all three cases is nonconformance. Why did the score shift at all? Our data is small: only 93 records. A very large dataset would show much smaller changes, or none at all.

Notes

1. Viktor Wase's original paper, "The Role of Base 10 in the Beale Ciphers," was published in the *Proceedings of the 3rd International Conference on Historical Cryptography.*
2. Data downloaded from the Nebraska Department of Motor Vehicles web portal. https://dmv.nebraska.gov/about/dmv-searchable-data.
3. A typical revenue management example would show a reversed pattern: too many 1s and too few 8s or 9s. For an excellent example, see Charles Carslaw's 1988 article in *The Accounting Review* entitled "Anomalies in Income Numbers: Evidence of Goal-Oriented Behavior."

PART III

Applications to Audit Practice

11

Professional Practice and Benford's Law

The majority of this book has been dedicated to the analytical usage of Benford's Law. In practice, auditors must often navigate questions about how Benford's Law fits into the audit process. How do we comply with audit and ethical standards? What kinds of engagements is it suited for? Where in the audit process do we deploy Benford's Law? This chapter is dedicated to these questions of professional practice.

11.1 Benford's Law Throughout the Audit Process

There's a lot of variety in audit practice. The general waterfall project style is fairly common: audits have phases for planning, execution (fieldwork), report writing, as well as post-project tasks like issue tracking and remediation. Benford's Law has some applications in each of these phases. The strongest use cases are probably in the risk assessment phase, though fieldwork is a strong second. Report writing and post-audit issue tracking are relatively uncommon use areas.

11.1.1 Audit Planning and Risk Assessment

Fundamentally, Benford's Law is a tool for identifying groups with unusual distributions of numbers. That makes it especially well-suited for risk assessment. Benford's Law doesn't replace the core of risk assessment activities such as talking to management, reviewing processes, and thinking critically about risk. Instead it augments those procedures by adding a quantitative check to an otherwise qualitative process.

Reviewing data should also be a central part of risk assessment. If the auditee has provided a dataset, Benford's Law can identify subsets of the data that the audit team might focus on. For example, in an audit of

DOI: 10.1201/9781003562238-14

sales commissions the audit team should expect to receive a population of commissions. Benford's Law could be used to identify departments, time periods, product lines, or other groups with unusual looking data. Those might be considered worthy of additional audit focus.

Internal audit's annual risk assessment could incorporate Benford's Law as a data point. This is not common and likely doesn't add significant value to most organizations. There are three reasons:

- Risk assessment is largely a qualitative exercise leveraging extensive professional judgment. Audit leaders interview high-level management (or perhaps conduct surveys), examine the enterprise's risk register or past risk events, and reflect on their conversations and knowledge of the business. These are not generally analytical procedures, and Benford's Law doesn't add significantly to this qualitative process.
- If the organization is leveraging data in their risk assessment, the range of risks being assessed is typically very broad. There is no single dataset to examine and no population to be constructed. Benford's Law isn't likely to address risks in any interesting or comprehensive way.
- A mature risk assessment function may have dedicated risk metrics and KPIs. In these cases, Benford's Law could potentially be used to supplement the existing risk metrics. Audit management could use Benford's Law to identify a group of transactions, a business unit, a vendor (etc.) with unusual pattern, but without a longer investigation, there's no way to know the substance of the risk. Since the risk assessment is supposed to identify risks (not anomalies), Benford's Law doesn't add much to this story.

Given these limitations, is there any opportunity to use Benford's Law? Absolutely. Many organizations have key risks or risk indicators that persist over many years. An audit team could use Benford's Law to assist with monitoring this data for underlying changes. For example, in an organization sensitive to shifts in inventory levels, the auditors would be likely to use inventory data in their risk assessment. They could augment that by incorporating Benford's Law into their assessment.

Benford's Law should be used whenever it's likely to provide value. If audit management believes Benford's Law is likely to reveal something interesting, it's fruitful to try. Nonetheless, it's likely that Benford's Law is more useful while planning an audit engagement than when conducting the annual risk assessment.

11.1.2 Fieldwork

The majority of people think about Benford's Law as a fraud test. Naturally, that means many practitioners think of Benford's Law as a test they apply in fieldwork. One key characteristic of Benford's Law is that it highlights unusual groups of data, not individual records that appear anomalous. That means we can't use it to reach a conclusion about individual records.

Benford's Law is often used in sample selection. There are two approaches. First, auditors might use Benford's Law on a large dataset, investigate the observed trends, and select individual records for their sample. This is the most common approach in traditional Benford's Law literature. For example, in a population of sales commissions paid, the auditor might observe too many records starting with "9," investigate those records, and see that a certain sales person has many commissions just underneath a key control. Some of those are selected as samples.

The second approach is to highlight groups of data for sample selection. For example, instead of selecting individual transactions as their samples, the auditors could select sales people and review their commissions. Benford's Law could be used on each sales person's data. The auditors would calculate a score for each sales person, find the most interesting, and include them in their sample. The key difference is using Benford's Law to select individual samples (in the above example) or to select groups in a stratified sample (in this example).

There is another use-case where auditors might use Benford's Law to provide negative assurance. Negative assurance means that the auditors haven't proved the records are correct, but they did not detect any irregularities. Benford's Law can be used to interrogate a dataset for irregularity. If the dataset conforms with Benford's Law, the auditors could document that and move on. Benford's Law should never be the single metric used to determine if an irregularity exists. There are many issues that will not be detected by Benford's Law (and many issues detected by Benford's Law may not be of interest for a particular audit). It's a single tool in the auditor's toolkit.

11.1.3 Report Writing and Issues Management

Benford's Law is unlikely to be a major component of either report writing or the post-audit issues management process. Auditors could potentially draw a bar plot or line plot demonstrating their usage of Benford's Law. That might be of interest in some cases. If an issue was detected through Benford's Law, then it provides a natural tool for monitoring that issue's remediation. For example, if Benford's Law was used to identify an accounts payable issue, the auditors might monitor that same data for changes over time. This is an example of the time series approaches described in Chapter 8. Since the issue was detected using Benford's Law, remediating the issue is expected to improve conformance.

11.2 Professional Standards

Auditors work under a variety of recognizant standards. In the United States, the International Professional Practices Framework (IPPF), published by the IIA and the basis for the Certified Internal Auditor certification, is broadly used in private organizations. The "Yellow Book" standards (formally called Generally Accepted Governmental Auditing Standards – GAGAS), published by the US Government Accountability Organization (GAO), are used in governmental auditing. There is a tapestry of other standards used outside the US, as well as at municipal and other organizations.

Benford's Law is an audit technique. Auditors must observe their recognizant standards by showing competence, skepticism, and other traits of ethical auditing. This section focuses on these ethical requirements.

11.2.1 Competence

The IIA and GAO both identify competence as the "knowledge, skills, and abilities" needed to conduct an engagement. If the audit team intends to use Benford's Law, they need the necessary skills to do so. The basics of Benford's Law are simple, but the well runs deep. Simple procedures require little skill or knowledge, but advanced techniques (such as designing machine learning algorithms or continuous monitoring applications) could require significant statistical or programming skills.

Simple techniques, such as visually inspecting a graph of the first digits against Benford's Law, require fairly little knowledge or skill. Basic familiarity with Excel functions and pivot tables would allow them to construct the needed graphs. A 1-hour seminar on Benford's Law (or sufficient time reading on the internet) would explain the basics adequately. Additional knowledge or experience is valuable for working expediently and interpreting charts more easily.

Leveraging goodness-of-fit scores requires at least one person on the team with a basic understanding of statistics. Most audit tools do not have Benford's Law built in. Those that do rarely have a goodness-of-fit score provided (except perhaps the Z-score, which is better left unused). Given the current state of the market, the audit team will need to calculate the score, which requires the ability to read a formula and translate it into an Excel formula. Basic statistical understanding helps interpret the score and identify risks. This is similar to how many teams handle sample size: the team has sampling tables provided by external auditors or a professional organization. The table is helpful for team members without statistical skills, but having at least one person with a knowledge of sampling theory provides flexibility and helps the team manage risks.

For advanced topics, the sky is the limit. An audit team that wants to use a Benford-like distribution (Chapter 6) to model their data requires someone comfortable with algebra (to modify Benford's Law formula) and computer programming (to search for the best values of the model). Designing a continuous monitoring application requires technical skills needed to build and manage data pipelines, as well as develop and maintain the monitoring solution itself.

11.2.2 Due Professional Care

Auditors are required to exercise due professional care. In essence, auditors are required to demonstrate good judgment in assessing the organizational context of their work (including industry trends, governance, and risks) and to use appropriate procedures to address that context. The GAO standards have similar concepts under different names.

Benford's Law should be used to accomplish a goal. The more the audit team understands about their business environment, risks, and audit objectives, the more useful Benford's Law will be. Consider two different scenarios:

- Auditors are generally aware of accounts payable risks including fraud, error, and non-compliance. They have not identified specific risks and aren't sure what about approval thresholds and other controls. They use Benford's Law, which uncovers numerous patterns. Since they don't know what's normal for their business and don't know what they are looking for, it's difficult to find actionable insights.
- Auditors are reviewing accounts payable. They have interviewed staff to understand the business process and narrowed their focus to a single risk. Each month, there is a flood of expenses on the last 2–3 business days related to employee travel. AP staff are concerned that detective controls are less effective in this period. Knowing this, the audit team uses Benford's Law. They use a time series approach (Chapter 8) and examine how well each day conforms to Benford's Law. They are able to quickly tell whether there are additional risks near the end of the month – and isolate employees with abnormal expenses.

Clearly, the auditors in the second scenario are in a stronger position. They exercised due professional care by understanding their organization, their risks, and designing work that meets their goals.

11.2.3 Professional Skepticism

Auditors should be inquisitive, but also critical about the information they are receiving. Benford's Law can be a great tool for demonstrating inquisitiveness. It can quickly identify patterns that teach us about the data and the business. Skepticism applies to the data being analyzed but also the results. Benford's Law should never be the sole factor in deciding that an issue exists. It should also not be the core evidence that fraud has been identified. Auditors should seek additional evidence that confirms their ideas. This could be substantive review of individual records, interviews with management, or additional analytics.

11.2.4 Quality of Evidence

Although IIA and GAO use different vocabulary, both require auditors to use high-quality evidence to support their conclusions. GAO asks for "sufficient and appropriate" evidence, while the IIA additionally asks for "reliable" information.

Data is "sufficient" when there is enough of it. Benford's Law is an analysis of full populations (or sub-populations). For visual inspection, there's no formula for a minimum number of records needed. The auditor is using their professional judgment to reach a conclusion about conformance to Benford's Law. No formula can capture professional judgment. Many Benford's Law experts have provided suggestions to use 100, 1,000, or more. These are matters of professional judgment and experience rather than statistics. Sufficiency is much clearer when using a goodness-of-fit score such as the D-score or Chi-squared. These metrics are all calibrated to accept a certain false-positive rate. Statisticians have calculated how much data is required for a certain degree of risk. Each metric will have its own threshold. See Chapter 5 for more details on each score.

Data is appropriate when it addresses the needs of the audit objective. Benford's Law does not introduce any new risks or concerns in this area. However, auditors should always be sure that they are using data that is germane to their audit. For example, in a cost recovery audit, the auditors typically review actual payments made by the organization to detect overpayments, duplicate payments, and other payment issues. Using Benford's Law to analyze contract amounts or invoice amounts would not be appropriate for this kind of audit, because they might not align with disbursements.

Reliability is a key concern for audit analytics – including Benford's Law. Thankfully, many kinds of data errors can be identified through Benford's Law. Auditors should feel comfortable using Benford's Law on data where reliability is either poor or unknown. They should be flexible in their interpretation: patterns may arise because of data quality, not because of the fraud or error they wish to detect. Of course, that also means that data quality concerns may prevent auditors from detecting the issues they desired to find in the first place. Completeness is one area that should be thought through. Benford's Law can't operate on data that isn't present, although in some cases it may be useful for identifying missing data.

11.3 Special Notes on Fraud

Benford's Law is best known as a tool for detecting potential fraud. This book has emphasized that Benford's Law will detect many kinds of irregularities, some of which are fraudulent. Since fraud is a common concern for auditors, it's worth looking specifically at this use case.

The majority of issues detected will not be fraud. This has been a theme throughout the book. Benford's Law is a general-purpose analytic test which can uncover many features of data including improper rounding, hard (or soft) limits, etc. Each of these could be caused by fraud or error, but is most likely not. An auditor would need to investigate further to decide whether any result is fraud. This is one of the tremendous values of using Benford's Law: the sheer variety of things that it can find. It may be inconvenient for audit teams that are highly focused on fraud.

Auditors increase the odds of finding fraud dramatically when looking for a specific kind of fraud. For example, revenue management schemes are a kind of financial statement fraud where management fraudulently reports higher revenues. These schemes have a kind of "fraud fingerprint" (in the words of Mark Nigrini) which we can observe with Benford's Law. We expect more numbers starting with 1, and fewer starting with high digits like 8 or 9. If we know what we are looking for, it's much easier to find something.

Finally, it is possible (but unlikely) that a clever fraudster could avoid Benford's Law. This is a classic example of *counterforensic* behavior. A fraudster who understood Benford's Law could manipulate financial reporting data, transactions, or other data to match Benford's Law. This would not be especially challenging. In practice, this is unlikely for several reasons. The fraudster would have to be knowledgeable in Benford's Law, which is unlikely. Additionally, they are more likely to purposefully evade common controls (like approvals, logs, etc.) rather than rare controls (like Benford's Law). While it is possible to evade detection by Benford's Law, it's not a common scenario an auditor or compliance professional would typically consider. Nonetheless, it may be a consideration when dealing with high-level threat actors such as foreign intelligence, professional hackers, or sophisticated fraud schemes.

12

CASE STUDY

IT Incident Management[1]

The majority of this book focuses on providing new techniques to use Benford's Law. Short demonstrations are provided to illustrate, briefly, how to apply techniques as they are being introduced. This chapter provides an in-depth case study demonstrating how, when, and why to use Benford's Law in an actual audit scenario. Fundamental techniques are emphasized: how to extract the first digits, visually examining the bar and line chart, etc. No statistical approaches are used. The next chapter is a case study that uses the same data but applies more advanced techniques.

Approximately 142,000 records from an IT company's incident management application (Service Now) will be analyzed. In this case study, we will first explore how Benford's Law fits into the auditors' project. Second, data will be processed and cleaned. Next, both the first-digit and two-digit tests will be used to explore actionable risks in the incident management data.

Sections 12.2 and 12.3 include considerable detail on implementing Benford's Law analyses using Microsoft Excel. If you are comfortable with Excel, either move briskly through that section or proceed directly to the analysis in Section 12.4.

12.1 Audit Background

Internal auditors are engaged in an audit of their company's incident management process. Incident management is the process by which IT issues are detected, worked, and resolved. This process could be used in an IT security context to refer to the detection and mitigation of security risks, but in other areas of IT, the most likely risks are service disruptions. The IT team needs to identify service disruptions

DOI: 10.1201/9781003562238-15

and resolve them quickly so that applications, services, and information assets are available to business users.

The audit team is currently in the planning stages of their audit. During the annual risk assessment, audit management determined there was a need for an audit of the incident management function. The audit team is now performing a more focused risk assessment to determine which specific risks and controls to evaluate. IT management has already provided a population: approximately 142,000 incident records from their incident management application, Service Now. Each record is a single incident. The record includes data about when and how an incident is reported, its resolution, and its eventual closure.

Although the audit team has not thoroughly identified their risks yet, they want to use Benford's Law to inform their audit procedures. They will use Benford's Law here in the planning phase to raise interesting questions to be addressed later. Benford's Law is likely to be the most interesting when the auditors already have some risks in mind. To help organize their thoughts, they outlined key risks and Benford's Law strategies in Table 12.1.

In addition to these risks, the auditors will be observant and watch for any other unusual results in their analysis.

Table 12.1 Benford's Law Opportunities

#	RISK DESCRIPTION	INDICATOR
1	Incidents are missing from the dataset. Perhaps they were never reported (a weakness in the incident detection controls) or were excluded from the data.	Missing data should look like one column (or a range of columns) having no data, and all other columns being slightly too high.
2	Incidents may be closed very quickly. This could indicate they were not legitimate incidents, were not entered timely (so that they were entered and resolved at the same time), or perhaps incident management staff closed them too quickly.	Easily detected without Benford's Law by looking at the time between incident creation and resolution. Benford's Law may reveal unnatural concentrations of these digits.
3	Management may have an incentive to close incidents quickly, perhaps under some pre-defined threshold, whether the incident is truly resolved or not.	This will look like the classic "threshold" result. There should be one column (or a range of columns) that is too high, with the columns immediately before or after being too low.

The auditors are also cognizant of following appropriate audit procedures. They decide that although Benford's Law does not need to be documented in their final planning memo, they should preserve their analysis in their audit files. Additionally, since this is a novel approach for their team, they will consider a "lessons learned" meeting to evaluate its success later. If Benford's Law proved valuable, it should be shared with the team for future usage.

12.2 Data Preparation

The incident data requires preparation before we can use Benford's Law. First, we need to decide on the column to analyze with Benford's Law. In this case, the auditors will create a new metric to analyze. Second, we need to extract digit frequencies.

12.2.1 Target Metric

Considering the risks the audit team is interested in, they decide that their target metric is the length of time between when an issue is opened and when it is resolved. The dataset does not have a column already populated with this value, but it does have the opening and resolution dates. These are represented as the columns "opened_at" and "resolved_at." One important consideration is that resolving an incident doesn't mean that the record is closed. The "resolved_at" column indicates when the incident was substantively resolved. The actual Service Now incident may remain open longer. For example, the team may return to a ticket at the end of the week, enter the resolved_at date (and any supporting information), then close the ticket.

12.2.2 Using Power Query to Resolve Data Formatting Challenges

The auditors need to calculate this "duration" column. Although the calculation is easy in Excel, they run into two challenges with the format of the data:

1. The data uses "?" to indicate a blank value. Any formula that expects a date or time will encounter an error because of this coding.

2. The data uses the UK datetime format (dd/mm/yyyy hh:mm), which is unfamiliar to the US-based audit team.

To resolve these problems, the auditors use both Excel and Power Query. Power Query is a feature built into Excel for ingesting and transforming data. The auditors manually remove the "?" character using Excel's "find and replace" feature. Power Query can ingest data from an Excel table, but not a normal tab. The auditors highlight the incident data and insert a table. Next, they select "From Table/Range" from the area marked "Get & Transform Data" in the Data tab. See Figure 12.1.

Excel will open Power Query in a new window. Changing the datetime format is as easy as right clicking on the desired column (in this case, opened_at and resolved_at). To change to a locale-specific format, select Change Type-> Using Locale and select the format the data currently uses. This is demonstrated in Figure 12.2. In this case, it's the UK English format.

To finish, select "Close and Load" in Power Query. Power Query will exit, process the change, and return a new tab to the original Excel document.

12.2.3 Creating the Metrics

The data has now been cleaned and is ready for use. Next, the auditors need to create their target metric. This is simple in Excel: it's the resolved_at column minus the opened_at column. The result is

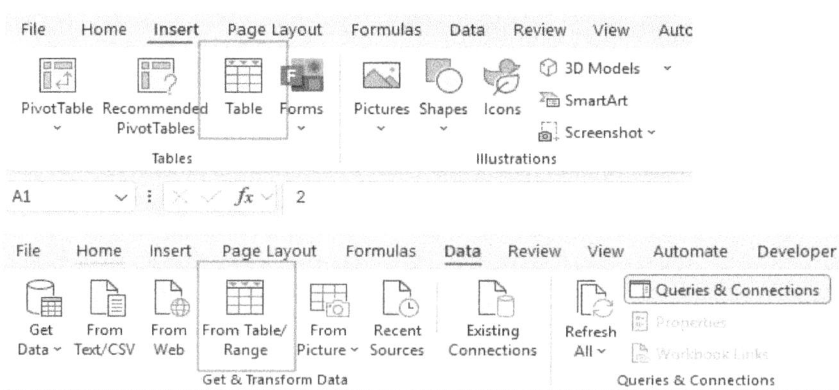

Figure 12.1 Location of "Insert Table" and "Get Data from Table/Range" features.

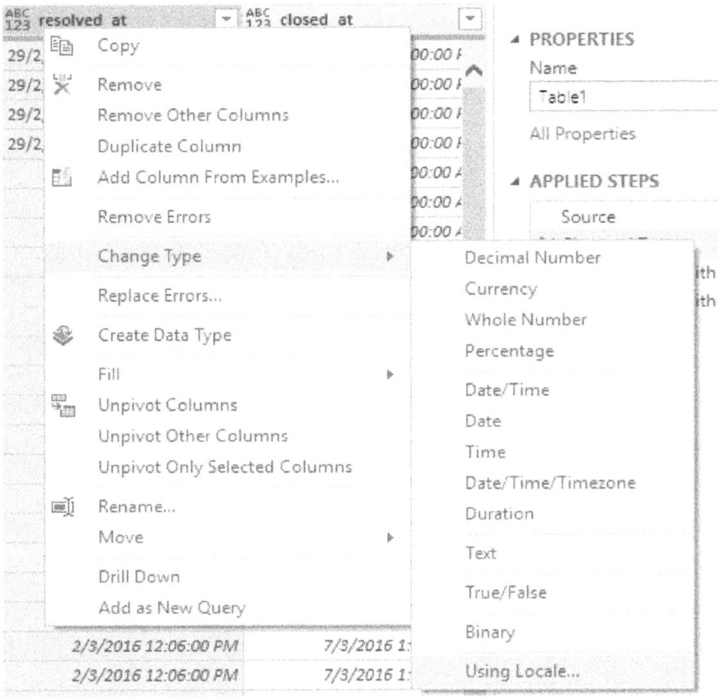

Figure 12.2 Changing the resolved_at column to use the US datetime format.

the number of days between the two columns. After reviewing their results, the auditors note two interesting things.

First, sometimes the formula returns an error. This happens because some incidents were not resolved when the report was run. The auditors could use a more sophisticated formula (for example, using if/then logic to only calculate the duration when both columns are completed). In this case, they manually delete the erroneous values when resolved_at is blank. These records will be removed from the analysis. The audit team considers their audit objectives and scope and determines that this is appropriate. Since the incidents are not yet completed, it's not logical to review their completion.

Second, the duration is sometimes *negative*. That means the incident was resolved *before* it was opened. It isn't clear what this means. Were these incidents reported after the fact, so the data is in-fact accurate? Should these be interpreted positively (perhaps it indicates that the IT team has excellent discipline about updating Service Now) or negatively (in that the events should have been reported earlier)?

The audit team decides to leave the negative values in. They will consider exploring the data with Benford's Law to see what they uncover. This issue will remain on their radar as they explore.

12.2.4 Extracting the First Digits

The last step in data preparation is to extract the first digit and first two digits of each duration value. Excel's LEFT() formula is the key mechanism here: it extracts the left-most characters of any value we pass it. For example, if the duration column says 5.1 days, then the left-most character is "5." This is almost exactly what we want. They create a new column called "FSD" (meaning "first-significant digit") with the formula:

$$FSD = \text{LEFT}\left(DurationColumn, 1\right)$$

After reviewing their results, the auditors see several unexpected values. In several cases, the formula returns "0" or a period. This happens when the Duration column is less than 1 (for example, the left-most character of 0.5 is "0"). The auditors solve this by multiplying the Duration column by 100,000 to ensure than no value is less than 1. The choice of number should always be a number like 10, 100, 1,000, etc. to avoid changing the first digits. This formula just shifts the decimal place over; it doesn't change the digits. Their new formula is:

$$FSD = \text{LEFT}\left(\left(Duration\,Column * 100000\right), 1\right)$$

Finally, the FSD is sometimes a hyphen ("-"). This happens when the Duration column is negative. The auditors had previously noted that some values were negative, but didn't adjust their formula here. To solve this problem, they use the absolute value of the Duration column. The absolute value removes negative signs, making negative numbers positive. The final formula is:

$$FSD = \text{LEFT}\left(\left(\text{ABS}\left(DurationColumn\right) * 100000\right), 1\right)$$

The FSD column now works exactly as expected. The auditors note that sometimes it returns 0. Even though Benford's Law ignores zeroes, this is acceptable. These are records where the incident was opened and resolved at exactly the same time. The auditors can note this observation and move on. During the next call with IT management, they can ask why some incidents are opened and resolved at exactly the same time.

They use almost exactly the same formula to extract the first two digits. The only change is that the LEFT() formula is adjusted to get the two left-most characters instead. They call this new column F2D (for "first two digits").

$$F2D = \text{LEFT}\left(\left(\text{ABS}\left(DurationColumn\right) * 100000\right), 2\right)$$

12.3 Implementing Benford's Law

The audit team will use both the first-digit test and the second-digit test. Excel's pivot table and chart features enable field auditors to develop these tests and visuals relatively easily.

12.3.1 Using Pivot Tables for the First Digit Test

The simplest analysis is the first-significant-digit test. The auditors previously decided to retain negative durations (cases where the incident was resolved before it was opened). Since they already created a new column with the first digit of each record, all that's left is to create a pivot table. Creating a pivot table in Excel involves highlighting the columns and selecting Data -> Insert Pivot (depicted in Figure 12.3). Although it's sufficient to include only the "FSD' column (which contains the first-significant digit), it's often advisable to include columns for filtering, grouping, etc. In this case, they select all columns.

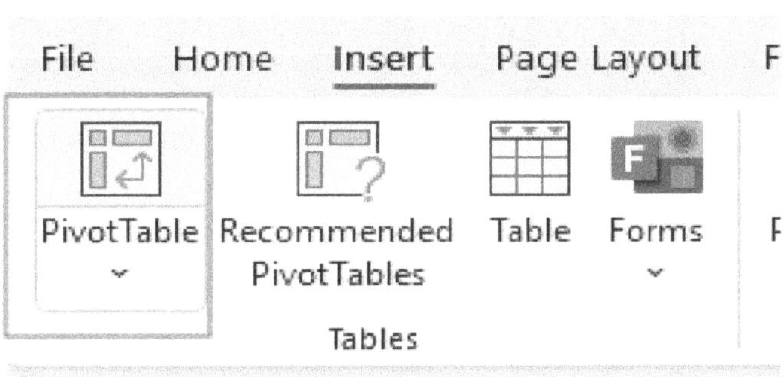

Figure 12.3 Creating a pivot table in Excel.

Creating the pivot table is similarly easy. Excel's interface asks what to include for each row, column, and the contents of each cell, as well as an option for filters. A simple Benford's Law analysis only requires two of these:

- In the "Rows" section, the auditors add their FSD column. The pivot table now has rows for each digit 1–9. If there were any other values, they would also appear here. This can be used as a sanity check to make sure no extraneous values exist.
- In the "Values" section, also add the FSD column. Excel will count the number of records with any value in the FSD column.

The result is a table that shows the number of records for each initial digit. Both the pivot table settings and the table itself are depicted in Figure 12.4.

The auditors can plot these values and should see the familiar shape of Benford's Law - or something like it. It's better to use the *percentage* of records that start with each digit, rather than the count. This is done by clicking on the down-arrow in the "Values" section and selecting "Value field settings." Excel will provide a window that allows you to configure several options about how values are

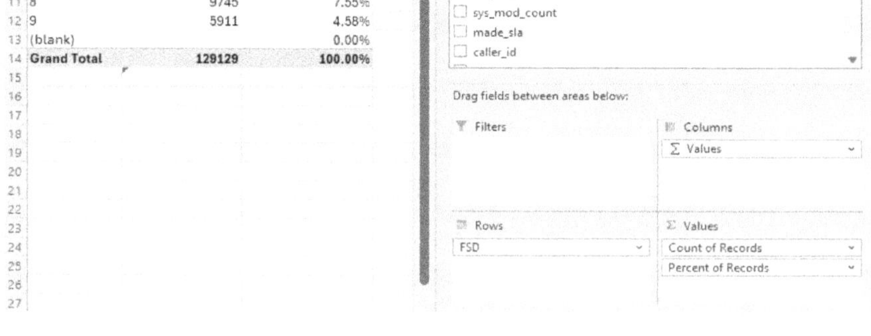

Figure 12.4 Pivot table with Benford's Law.

shown. The desired option is called "Show value as" and the auditors select "percent of the column total." Excel now calculates what percentage of records start with each digit. An identical exercise can be done for the two-digit test.

Excel's pivot tables make it a snap to quickly perform this analysis on filtered subsets. For example, the audit team could include a filter on the location field to test individual locations. The audit team is currently operating at a high level and does not desire this level of detail, so they do not perform any filtered analyses.

It's often easier to visualize the results of Benford's Law. In this case, the auditors might choose to use a combination chart (or combo chart) where bars are used to represent the frequencies they observed in their data, while the line is used to represent Benford's Law. Benford's Law can be easily calculated in Excel using the formula in Chapter 2. Steps for creating this chart are omitted. These visuals (and a discussion of the results) appear in the next section.

12.4 Analysis and Results

Figure 12.5 shows the audit team's results for both the first-digit and two-digit tests. Visually, this doesn't match Benford's Law. The first-digit test

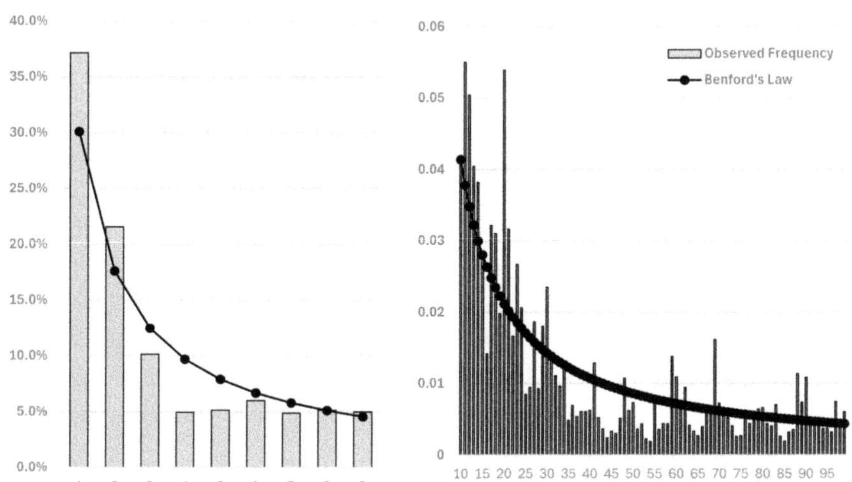

Figure 12.5 First digit and first two digit tests of incident data.

is fairly straightforward: 1–2 is too high, and there is a small spike at 8. The two-digit test has numerous anomalies, most notably:

- Too much data throughout most of the 10-range (11–14, 17–18)
- Large spikes at 20–21.
- Too much data throughout 57–60
- A noticeable spike at 69
- Too much data throughout 86–90

Each of those observations from the two-digit test is a chance to investigate in more detail, but the audit team should start with the high-level results in the first-digit test. There are at least two patterns in the chart: the 1–2 range, and the spike at 8. The concentration of data in the 1–2 range could suggest issues are being closed sooner than Benford's Law expects. This also causes the other columns to be too low. It isn't clear whether this is due to some limit in the data (such as a monitoring control or KPI), or something else. There's no obvious explanation for the spike at 8. Perhaps there is a ceiling here that prevents issues from lingering open too long.

While the audit team could delve into those issues, they could instead turn their attention to the two-digit test. There are so many bars here that it's unwise to focus on each individual bar and comprehensively examine all of them. Instead, the audit team should look for patterns such as ranges that are too high, large spikes, or periodic increases/decreases.

They decide to first focus on the largest spike at 20 and the lesser spike at 21. They include both, because they think that the two are likely related. They filter the population of Service Now incidents to only those where the first two digits are 20 or 21. There are about 11,000 incidents in this range. After manually looking at the data, the audit team identifies two patterns.

- First, about ⅓ of these records were closed immediately after the 200-day mark. They consider the possibility that management is monitoring the aging of incidents and intervenes around this time.
- Second, about 800 incidents were resolved in less than 1 minute after being opened. 800 out of 11,000 isn't a large number, but the audit team recalls this is one of their key risks.

Next, they focus on the spike at 69. This spike stands alone. It isn't surrounded by other columns that are too high. Dramatic single spikes sometimes signal significant duplication, or perhaps a floor or ceiling. 1,300 out of the 2,100 incidents starting with 69 were all closed in either 0.00069 or 0.0069 days. This corresponds to exactly 1 minute or 10 minutes. This heavy duplication likely causes the spike. The auditors note this issue and move on.

12.5 Wrapping Up

The audit team has used Benford's Law to examine their data. They are not currently in fieldwork; they are using Benford's Law during audit planning to identify actionable risks or patterns. What have they found?

First, the auditors noted there are incidents with negative durations. These are cases where the incident appears to have been resolved *before* it was opened. This was detected when extracting the first digit from each duration (the first character would have been a minus sign). It's unclear whether this is a data entry problem, a facet of Service Now's reporting, or a legitimate problem. The auditors can ask management more in their next call.

Second, some incidents are resolved at the same time they are opened. This was detected when extracting the first digit of each duration: 0 has no first-significant digit. It's unclear whether these were opened in error, are subject to some kind of batch processing, or were closed intentionally for malicious reasons.

Third, there is a soft limit around 200 days. Benford's Law expects data to be distributed in a relatively smooth way. In this case, it has detected too many records where the incident was closed around the 200-day mark. This could be a result of monitoring controls (perhaps management pays more attention to incidents around this time period). Any legitimate pattern could also be caused by illegitimate activities. For example, management may have incentives to close issues around this 200-day mark whether they are resolved or not.

Fourth, they noted that many issues are closed in 1 or 10 minutes. These are distinct from the incidents that are closed at the same time they are opened. At face value, these are less likely to be automated activities. They may have been opened in error. Alternatively, perhaps these issues were low risk and could be closed quickly.

The auditors can follow up on all of these during fieldwork. Notably, these observations could substantiate 2 of the 3 risks the auditors identified in their risk matrix (Table 12.1). They did not observe anything to suggest that incidents are missing from the dataset. Benford's Law is unlikely to detect a small number of missing records. This can be framed as negative assurance. The audit team deployed analytics to evaluate a potential risk. They did not find evidence for that risk, but they can't prove it isn't there.

Note

1. This dataset was published by Claudio Amaral, Marcelo Fantinato, and Sarajane Peres and made available by the University of California-Irvine's Machine Learning Repository. It can be downloaded from https://archive.ics.uci.edu/dataset/498/. Although the dataset here comes from Amaral et al., the audit narrative is the author's own. It is intended to provide an educational context for performing this kind of analysis.

13

Case Study

Statistical Techniques

Most chapters in this book introduce new techniques for leveraging Benford's Law. Since their goal is to introduce a new idea, those chapters include short case studies to briefly demonstrate how to use the techniques in that chapter. This chapter is a detailed case study that ties together many individual concepts. The prior detailed case study focused on fundamental (non-statistical) approaches. In this case study, the focus will be on applying quantitative or statistical techniques.

ServiceNow is a tool for managing different IT and ticketing systems. The data for this case study is approximately 142,000 incidents for an IT services company.[1] The auditors want to use more advanced statistical concepts to improve their audit planning. They want to use Benford's Law to select high-risk groups for their audit. To accomplish this, they will leverage a goodness-of-fit score (the D score) to score groups. Power BI will be leveraged to automate the calculations. Finally, they will create a time series and position themselves for continuous monitoring.

13.1 Audit Background

An internal audit team is engaged in an audit of their company's incident management process.[2] They have collected incidents from their company's incident management system, ServiceNow. Their data has roughly 142,000 records. In the previous chapter, they used a simple Benford's Law approach to uncover numerous interesting questions.

Currently, they are faced with two questions. First, how can they select meaningful groups to target for their audit? They could select a random sample of incidents to review, but with limited audit resources, random sampling may not be the most effective strategy. They would

DOI: 10.1201/9781003562238-16

prefer to group the incidents by vendor, employee reporting the issue, incident category, etc. and identify meaningful groups to include in their scope. Second, they would like to lay the groundwork for continuous monitoring.

13.2 Benchmarking with a Goodness-of-Fit Score

Goodness-of-fit scores (Chapter 5) provide a way to measure how close a dataset is to Benford's Law. In order to meet their goals, the audit team will need a score that they can use to identify high-risk areas of concern, as well as develop a continuing monitoring application. The audit team considers their needs when selecting an appropriate score:

- They will not be performing a statistical hypothesis test, so it's not necessary to select a score with known critical values.
- They do want to be certain they have enough data to reach a meaningful conclusion ("*sufficient evidence*" in the words of their audit standards).

Although they don't need a score with critical values for hypothesis testing purposes, those scores allow them to know if they have sufficient data in a quantitative way. They decide that a score with a known critical value is important. Accordingly, they choose the D-score. Why? The MAD score doesn't have known critical values, so they could not have been certain they have sufficient data. They could choose the Chi-squared score, but the D-score is more efficient (it requires less data to reach an equally valid conclusion). The D-score is the most efficient tool to meet their needs.

The D-score[3] is relatively easily calculated in Excel. Recall that the formula (from Chapter 5) is:

$$D = \sqrt{\#\, of\ records} \times \sqrt{\sum_{d=1}^{9} (Frequency\ of\ d - Frequency\ expected\ by\ Benford's\ Law)^2}$$

where *d* is the digit.

The auditors will prepare their data as described in Chapter 12. Their key metric is the amount of time between when an issue was opened and when it was resolved. They will need to exclude records that are not yet resolved, as well as records where the issue was opened and resolved at exactly the same moment. During their calculations, they also notice that some records have a *negative* duration: the incident was resolved before it was created. They also exclude these from the analysis. This exclusion isn't for statistical purposes (Benford's Law would be just fine including them), but because they seem to represent a different set of questions for management.

The result is that 115,593 records remain. Figure 13.1 shows their initial Benford's Law analysis.

Calculating the D-score is relatively easy, but requires several steps. Table 13.1 shows these calculations occurring. The overall D-score is 34.36. The critical value for 95% confidence is 1.330, so in this case, the auditors could safely (and easily) conclude that this data doesn't follow Benford's Law. This doesn't matter, because they aren't interested in performing a statistical hypothesis test. However, it's useful to build intuition about just how big 34.36 is: it's about 30 × the accepted limit.

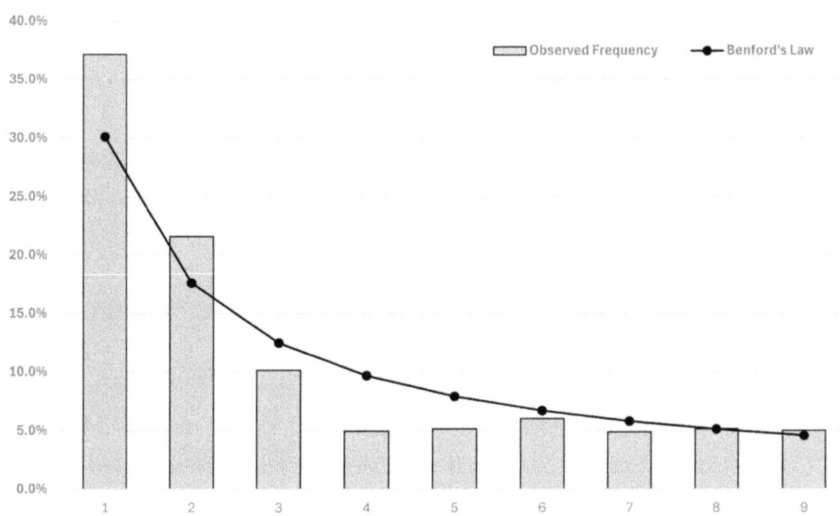

Figure 13.1 Naïve Benford's Law analysis of service now incident durations.

Table 13.1 Example of Calculating D-Score in Excel

DIGIT	BENFORD'S LAW	OBSERVED FREQUENCY	DIFFERENCE	DIFFERENCE SQUARED
1	30.1%	37.1%	–0.070	0.00495
2	17.6%	21.6%	–0.040	0.00157
3	12.5%	10.1%	0.024	0.00055
4	9.7%	5.0%	0.047	0.00223
5	7.9%	5.2%	0.028	0.00076
6	6.7%	6.0%	0.007	0.00005
7	5.8%	4.9%	0.009	0.00008
8	5.1%	5.1%	0.000	0.00000
9	4.6%	5.0%	–0.004	0.00002
		Sum of differences squared		0.01021
		Square root of the above sum		0.10106
		Square root of the number of records		339.99
		D-score		34.36

The steps to this calculation are:

1. For each digit 1–9, calculate the percentage of records that start with that digit ("Observed Frequency" column) and the expected value from Benford's Law ("Benford's Law" column).
2. For each digit 1–9, subtract the observed and expected values ("Difference" column). It doesn't matter which column comes first in the formula.
3. For each digit 1–9, square those differences ("Difference Squared" column). This removes the negative sign, but it also provides a bigger penalty for large variances.
4. Add up all of those squared differences.
5. Calculate the square root of the number of records (in our case, the square root of 115,593 is 339.99).
6. Multiply the square root of the number of records (339.99) by the sum of squared differences (approximately 0.1). The result is 34.36: this is our D-score. Note that values in the table are rounded.

These calculations can be easily put into an Excel template, so that the only change is to the "Observed Frequency" column. Alternatively, it can be implemented in Power BI, Python, SQL, or other solutions.

13.3 Optimizing Benford's Law

The auditors have calculated their D-score. It's 34.36, which is significantly beyond the critical value of 1.330. Although the auditors weren't interested in conducting a statistical hypothesis test, they could be reasonably sure that this data doesn't follow Benford's Law. That's also fairly clear from Figure 13.1. The initial digits 1 and 2 are too frequent and the curve slopes more quickly than Benford's Law allows.

Since the auditors will be using their D-score extensively (eventually building a continuous monitoring application), they decide to optimize Benford's Law for their use case. This will help reduce false positives and increase the fit provided by Benford's Law. They adopt the parameterization approach described in Chapter 6. Parameterization for Benford-like distributions involves introducing two new variables (*P* and *Q*) into the familiar Benford's Law formula:

$$Probability\ (D) = log\left(1 + \frac{1}{P + D^{Q}}\right) * N$$

The auditors aren't sure what values of *P* and *Q* are appropriate. They decide to use a Python library to help locate values of *P* and *Q*. After running the script, they identify a useful solution where $P = 1.0$ and $Q = 1.6$. Increasing *Q* above one means that the curve will have a sharper descent before flattening out, which also matches their observation. Increasing *P* above 1 means that Benford's Law has less of peak, which moderates the effect of the large *Q* value. This may not be an optimal solution, but it's a significant improvement. It's likely that they could further optimize their fit, perhaps reduce the remaining error considerably.

The "*N*" term at the end of the formula is a normalization factor. If the auditors performed the formula without *N*, their percentages wouldn't add up to 100%. This term is a reminder to re-state each result as the percentage of the total. This is described in more detail in Chapter 6.

Figure 13.2 shows their new Benford-like curve. Their new, more optimal, curve has a D-score of 19.99. This is a significant improvement from the prior score of 34.36. If they were using a statistical hypothesis test, this would still be rejected by Benford's Law. Any statistical test is going to be picky for a dataset of this size. There

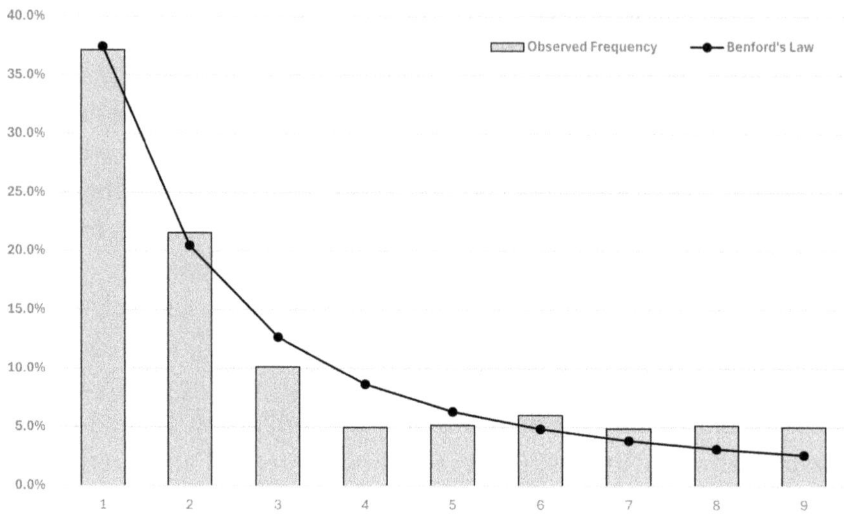

Figure 13.2 Benford-like Law for incident durations.

should be little random error, so the statistical test expects the data to match very closely.

13.4 Benford's Law in Power BI

Benford's Law has now been tailored to the audit team's data. Their first goal is to identify groups with the worst conformance to Benford's Law. These are the groups they would want to target in an audit of the incident management process. This is a natural complement to the simple Benford's Law analysis performed in Chapter 12.

The calculations could be performed in Excel. That would require some tedious work, and the resulting spreadsheet wouldn't be flexible. If the auditors wanted to explore different groupings, they would have to reperform their calculations. The solution is to use Power BI (or another data visualization tool) to build a more flexible solution. This section describes how to implement the parameterized Benford's Law in Power BI, how to use Power BI to automatically perform these calculations, and how to build flexible exploration features.

Experienced Power BI users might skip or scan this section and proceed to 13.4.

13.4.1 Creating Benford's Law in Power BI

First, we need a way to represent Benford's Law in our data. Benford's Law doesn't depend on our data: it's just a calculation based on our formula. Conceptually, Benford's Law is an expected frequency calculated for each initial digit. That means we need a table with two things: each potential digit, and the frequency expected by Benford's Law.

Power BI is typically intended to read data from another source. We can create a new table in the model view: the same place where we can view tables and relationships. The Home tab has an option for creating a new table. If the auditors have already calculated their expected frequency using Benford's Law, they can manually construct the table like this:

```
Digits =
DATATABLE (
    "Digit", INTEGER,
    "Expected Value", DOUBLE,
    {
        { 1, 0.3744 },
        { 2, 0.2046 },
        { 3, 0.1267 },
        { 4, 0.0865 },
        { 5, 0.0631 },
        { 6, 0.0484 },
        { 7, 0.0385 },
        { 8, 0.0315 },
        { 9, 0.0263 }
    }
)
```

Observe that the auditors are using the parameterized Benford-like values they calculated in Section 13.2.

The DATATABLE() function creates a new table. The first column is the first-significant digit, which includes all digits 1–9. That doesn't mean our data actually includes each of these digits, but we do need to calculate Benford's Law for each. The second column is the expected frequency of each digit. In this case, the auditors calculated it outside of Power BI (perhaps in Excel) and hard coded the values here.

Alternatively, they could have used a calculated column to automatically create those values. The formula to do this is more complicated, because the Benford-like distribution requires normalization. They would have first created a table with just the Digit column. For simplicity, let's say they use two calculated columns. The first calculates the percentages using their selected value of P and Q:

```
Percent_not_normalized = LOG10(1+(1/(1+Digits
[Digit]^1.6)))
```

The second column normalizes the results so that the total is 100%. It's the expected frequency for each row divided by the total:

```
Percent_Normalized =
DIVIDE (
    'Digits'[Percent_not_normalized],
    CALCULATE (
        SUM ( 'Digits'[Percent_not_normalized] ),
        ALL ( 'Digits' )
    )
)
```

Regardless of which method they use, the auditors now have a table with *both* the digits and the expected frequency.

13.4.2 Extracting Digit Frequencies in Power BI

Power BI can read data from a multitude of sources: databases, cloud-based data warehouses, third-party applications via API, and more. In this example, the auditors have their incident data in an Excel document saved locally. Power BI can read that, too. Power BI uses Power Query to read-in data. This process is identical in Excel and may be familiar to some auditors.

In the report view, simply go to Get Data and select the kind of data source you are reading (in this case, an Excel file). Power BI will prompt you for the location of the file. It's as easy as finding

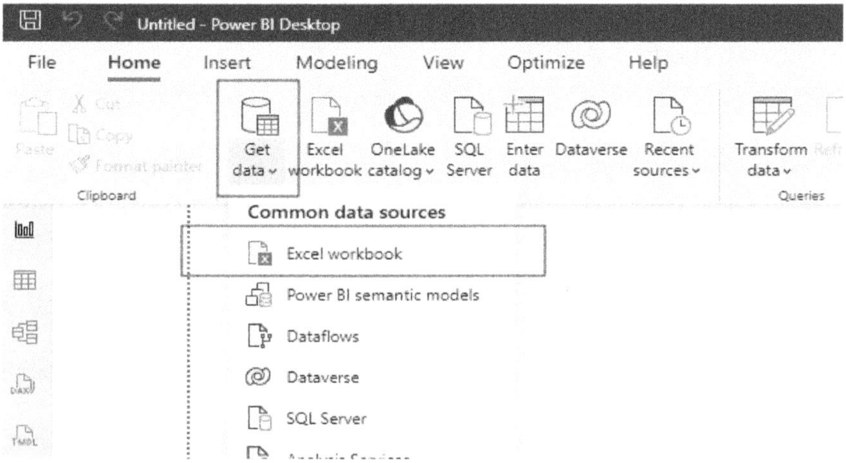

Figure 13.3 Importing an Excel Workbook in Power BI.

the right file and opening it. Figure 13.3 shows the location of this option. Power Query has a powerful suite of tools for manipulating data, cleaning errors, and many other tasks, but none are needed in this example.

Power BI now has access to the incident data. The auditors need to extract the first digit frequencies from the duration column just like they did in the prior chapter. The process is largely the same. Power BI allows for the creation of calculated columns: formulas that are calculated for every row in the data. Since the auditors previously did this work in Excel in the prior chapter, they could easily read in their first-significant digits from their Excel file. Alternatively, they could create a calculated column with a formula like this:

```
FirstDigit = LEFT(ABS('snow bl'[Duration: Open to
Resolved]*100000), 1)
```

This is similar to the formulas seen for Excel in prior chapters. The "duration" value (the time difference between when an issue is created and its resolution) is multiplied by a large number like 100,000. This doesn't change the first digit, but does move the decimal place to account for small values. ABS() is the absolute function, which is useful for removing negative signs. Finally, the auditors use LEFT() to retrieve the first digit.

13.4.3 Joining Data Sets

The auditors have both the expected values from Benford's Law and the first digits from their data. One step is still needed before they can do their analysis: the two datasets need to be connected. Consider two different tabs in an Excel worksheet. Auditors often use XLOOKUP or VLOOKUP (or INDEX/MATCH) to reference values on another worksheet. Power BI has the same concept.[4]

Power BI allows this kind of data management in the model view. The model view shows all tables (similar to Excel's worksheets), as well as the connections between them. In this case, the auditors have two tables: Digits (representing their digits and the expected frequency) and Incidents (representing the incident data that was just uploaded). Connecting them is easy. Just like VLOOKUP the auditors need a column in common to match on. The first-significant digit in the incidents data is expected to match one of the digits in the digit table. The connection is as easy as clicking on one column and dragging onto the other. Power BI will ask for some settings (depicted in Figure 13.4).

The default values should be appropriate for this usage. Notably, the relationship is *one-to-many* (or *many-to-one* depending on which table the auditors started on). This means that one record in the digits table corresponds to many records in the incidents data. For example, the digit "1" (one record in the digits table) likely corresponds to many thousands of records where the first digit of the duration column is "1."

13.4.4 The Analysis

Finally, the auditors are ready to conduct their analysis. Creating the familiar column-and-line charts seen throughout this book is a breeze. First, they need to select the kind of figure they want from the Visualizations pane. Power BI calls this a "line and stacked column chart." Power BI will populate the page with the chart selected. Just like Excel's pivot tables, the auditors need to select the columns they want to use. Figure 13.5 shows these settings.

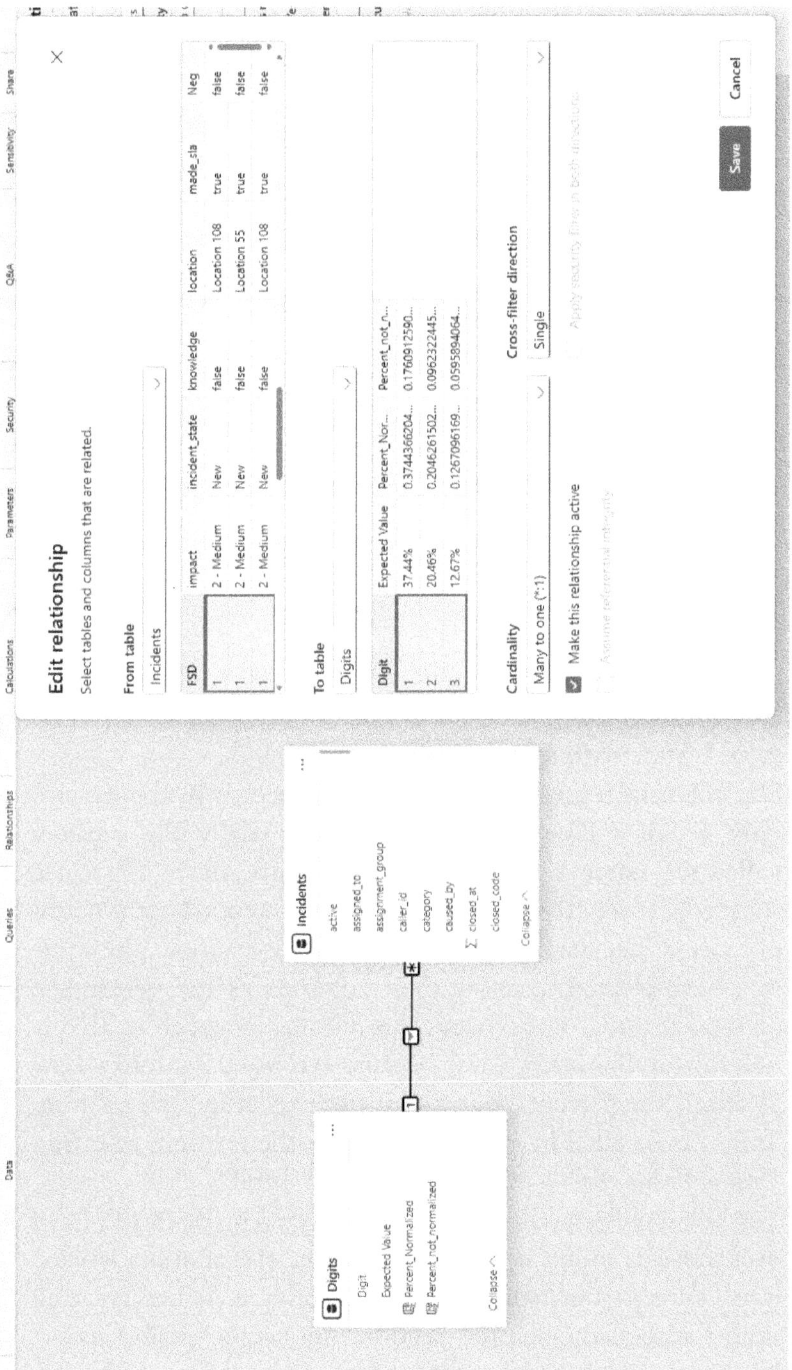

Figure 13.4 Relationships between tables in Power BI.

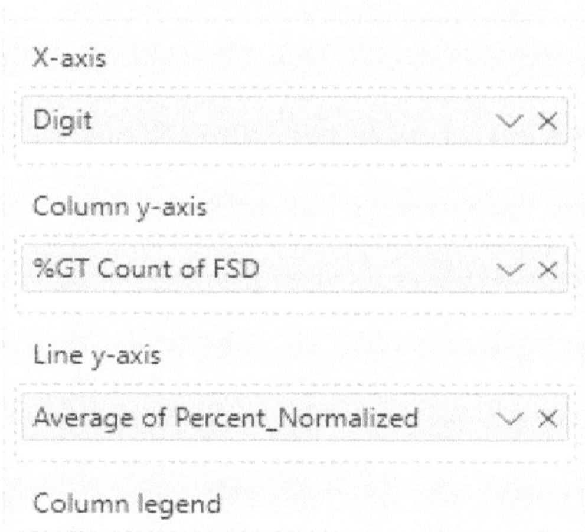

Figure 13.5 Example of dropping Power BI fields into charts.

They are mostly intuitive enough, but Power BI has some of its own interesting features:

- The X-axis is the Digits column, which represents the digits 1-9. This ensures that a bar will exist for every digit, even if no records start with that digit.
- The columns represent the number of records in the Service Now incident data that start with that digit. The auditors called this column "FSD" (for "first-significant digit"). Once selected, Power BI will create columns representing the count of records that start with that digit. In this example, the auditors have elected to show their columns as the percentage of total records, rather than the number of records. This is helpful for Benford's Law, because we used Benford's Law to tell us the percentage of records to expect in each column. This is controlled by right-clicking on the column, selecting "Show Value As" -> "Percent of Grand Total."
- The line represents the proportion expected by Benford's Law. This value is found in the Digits table. The auditors labeled it as "Percent_normalized" in the prior step. When creating their formulas in the prior section, this was a sensible name: it distinguished between the percentages before and after

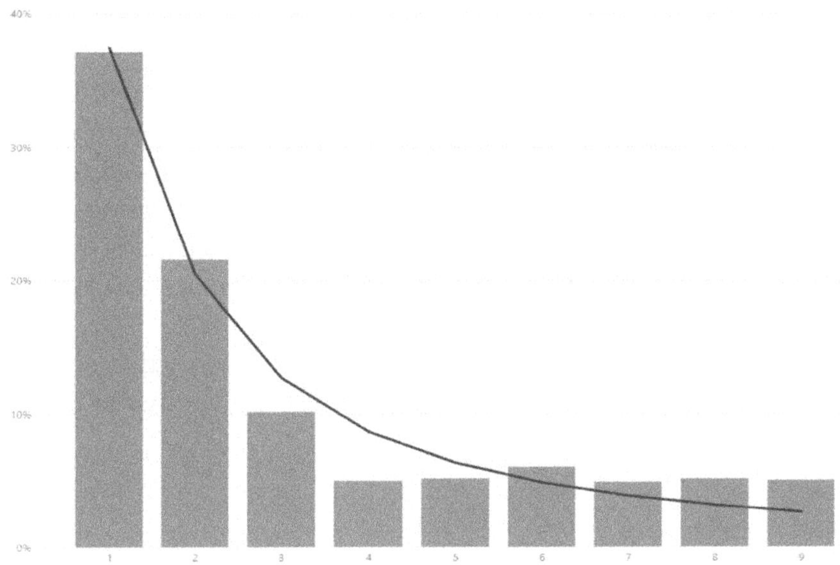

Figure 13.6 Simple Benford's Law figure in Power BI.

being normalized. Here, the name is confusing. They can easily change it by right-clicking on the column and selecting "Rename for this visual."

Power BI has a rich feature set with many options. The auditors might want to do a variety of other things to their data, but this is the minimum. The result is Figure 13.6, which shows the familiar Benford's Law chart.

This may seem like more steps (and more work) than using Excel. Just like Excel, it becomes a habit and can be done very quickly once you are familiar with Power BI. Additionally, Power BI allows quick changes to visuals. It's easy to filter the data (perhaps for different time periods, IT staff, or other characteristics). The results are immediately visible with no additional recalculation needed.

13.5 Finding High Risk Groups

The auditors have laid the foundations of all their analysis. The basics are completed. Their next goal is to locate high-risk groups within the incident dataset. This will help focus the audit work on the most important areas. More than any other technique, this is often highly valuable in the planning stages of an audit.

To accomplish this, they will assign a score to each subset. In this example, it will be the D-score. This is simply a Power BI measure. A measure is different from a calculated column. A calculated column results in a new value for each record – just like a column in Excel. A measure summarizes many records. Excel formulas like SUM() do this: they read multiple rows and return a single number. The formula for the D-score has already been discussed.

The D-score is based on the percentage of records that actually start with each digit. The auditors can make their life easier by encapsulating this in a measure:

```
Observed % =
DIVIDE(
    COUNTROWS('Incidents'),
    CALCULATE(
        COUNTROWS('Incidents'), REMOVEFILTERS(Digits)
)
    )
```

At this point, the remaining calculations can be completed. The auditors have the actual percentage of records for each digit (in the above measure) and the expected percentage from Benford's Law (in their Digits table). What remains is to combine them into the D-score:

```
D (Cho-Gaines) =
SQRT(
    SUMX(
        Digits,
        POWER(
                [Observed %] - Digits[Expected Value],
            2
        )
    )
) * sqrt(COUNTROWS(Incidents))
```

The D score allows the auditors to quickly find high-risk subsets in their data. Figure 13.7 shows a scatterplot. The two axes are the number of records and the D-score: higher D scores mean a worse

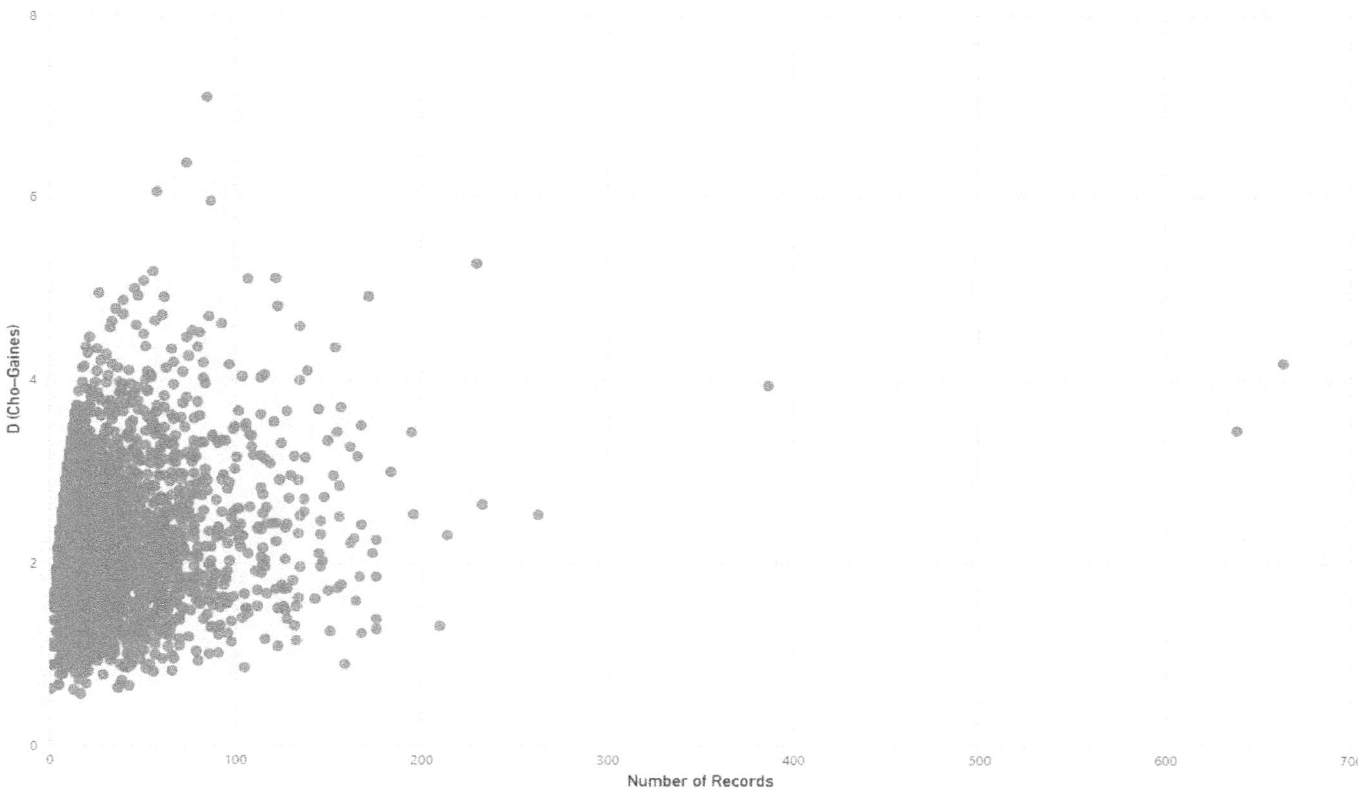

Figure 13.7 Power BI scatterplot comparing the D-score and number of records for each Caller.

fit to Benford's Law. Each dot represents a single caller reporting an incident.

The auditors focus on the top-most point. That has the biggest D score, and therefore the worst fit to Benford's Law. It also has a fair number of records: 85 incidents reported by this user. That's enough for a valid conclusion from the D-score, although they aren't interested in that usage. The column-and-line plot reveals that this data significantly varies from Benford's Law: 91% of incidents reported by this user have a duration that starts with "2"! Manually examining the data, the auditors see some more specific patterns. A large number of records for this reporter are closed around 210–240 days. Moreover, those records are being closed by the same handful of IT personnel. This gives them an auditable pattern – something to explore in detail in fieldwork.

Although the Power BI dashboard took a moment to set up, it provided two key benefits. First, it allows the auditors to quickly reperform this analysis on different groupings. Previously, they looked at the caller who reported the incident, and they found a caller with a seemingly greater risk than others. They could also look at vendor groupings, product or service groupings, incident categories, or nearly any other column present in the data. It takes only a few seconds to change the field in the Power BI chart. Second, Power BI provided a way to identify the highest-risk group in each analysis. In the prior example, the audit team found a single caller with the highest D score and were able to dig-in to identify specific risk indicators. This would have taken more time in Excel.

13.6 Time Series and Continuous Monitoring

The audit team has one final goal. They want to use their Power BI dashboard to monitor compliance with Benford's Law over time. Power BI makes this a snap. The auditors can just create a new visualization. This time, they select a line chart. The y-axis will be the D-score: higher scores mean worse conformance to Benford's Law. They need a date for the x-axis. The incident data has several dates to choose from, but the audit team selects the resolution date (resolved_at). Their line chart is depicted in Figure 13.8.

Power BI can group the data daily, monthly, quarterly, or yearly by default. This figure shows a monthly Benford's Law analysis. The trend is fascinating: Benford's Law compliance is overall poor until

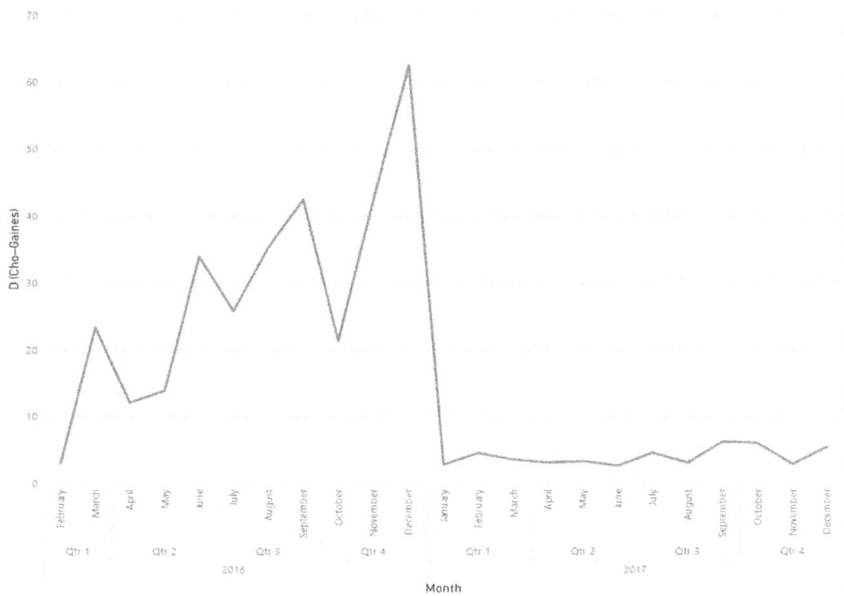

Figure 13.8 Line chart showing D-score over time.

December 2016. In December, it peaks with an incredible D-score of 62.5! Immediately after December, it falls to a stable range of 2–3.

This is a good example of using the D-score, but not using critical values. Likely every month will fail a statistical hypothesis test. The D-scores observed here are always bigger than the critical value. If we used that strict hypothesis test, every month would be flagged. That isn't the auditors' goal. They want a monitoring solution. The D-score provides a metric that can be monitored over time. In this case, we see the metric spiking in one time period: that's a red flag that December is a period we should audit. Additionally, we see the entire pattern change in December. That's an indicator that something fundamentally changed within the business process.

The auditors can probe deeper during their planning phase. In December, about 98% of all incidents resolved had a duration starting with "2." There are 5,200 incidents resolved in December. Nearly all of them were open for 200–240 days. The auditors validate this by looking at the opening date: nearly all of them were opened in April and May 2016. Why were so many incidents opened in April and May? Why did they all get closed in the same time period in December? The auditors could continue to use Power BI to dig deeper into root causes. Perhaps the majority of these were reported by the same caller, resolved by the same IT staff, included the same technologies, etc.

Continuous monitoring is easily accomplished in Power BI. The precise steps change depending on the auditor's IT environment, licensing, and other factors. Speaking broadly, Power BI has features for subscriptions and alerts. Subscriptions can be used to send regular updates on the status of a report. For example, the auditors may configure the subscription to send them the latest D-score once a month. Alerts continuously monitor the data and send an e-mail once a certain threshold is met. For example, the auditors could configure the alert to notify them if the D score ever increases by more than 10%, or if it ever surpasses 4.

13.7 Wrapping Up

In this chapter, the audit team used Benford's Law to continue their analysis of their organization's IT incident data. They wanted to use Benford's Law for two purposes: (1) identifying high-risk groups within their data, and (.) developing a continuous monitoring application. These use cases required more calculations than Excel could conveniently deliver, so they decided to use Power BI instead. Power BI required some initial setup (importing data, creating calculations, etc.), but the result is a highly flexible and powerful automated dashboard.

The auditors were successful in both of their goals. The Power BI dashboard allows them to quickly check different kinds of groupings such as the incident category, risk rating, and other categorizations. They found an interesting pattern when grouping the data by caller ID: one particular caller had a high D-score. Upon further examination, the auditors saw that 91% of their incidents had a duration starting with "2." Additionally, their records were overwhelmingly closed in the 210–240-day time period and by the same small set of IT personnel.

Their second was continuous monitoring. As part of this development, the auditors built a time series showing how the D-score changes over time (based on the resolution date). They observed an interesting trend: prior to December, the data generally didn't follow Benford's Law, but after December, it became much closer and well-behaved. December itself had a very poor fit. Looking closer, they discovered that nearly all the incidents closed in December had durations that started with the same digit. Indeed, nearly all of the records were opened in the prior April or May and suddenly closed in December. They decide to ask management about these trends.

Continuous monitoring is enabled by Power BI and Benford's Law, supplemented by a goodness-of-fit score. The auditors can configure their data to refresh regularly, ingesting new data based on the issue resolution date. Power BI can be configured to either send regularly scheduled updates or tell them when the goodness of fit score shows unusual behavior.

Notes

1. This is the same dataset from Chapter 12. It was published by Claudio Amaral, Marcelo Fantinato, and Sarajane Peres, and made available by the University of California-Irvine's Machine Learning Repository. The use case and business purposes are the author's own.
2. Incident management is described in more detail in the prior chapter.
3. This is the modified D-score from James Morrow. See details in Chapter 5. It is modified to account for the number of records, which is what allows us to construct the critical values.
4. Readers with database experience will recognize this as a join.

Appendix: Deriving Benford's Law

This book is not a mathematics textbook. It's written for auditors and analytics professionals who want to use Benford's Law in practice, without needing an advanced math background. Introductory content is intentionally non-mathematical so that any field auditor could use it. Still, some readers may wonder: *Where does Benford's Law come from?* This appendix gives a straightforward explanation. It's not a formal proof, but an illustration demonstrating how Benford's Law arises naturally from our numbering system.

I present two different approaches here:

1. An algebraic approach, showing how the formula can be built step by step from some basic notions.
2. A visual approach, showing how the logarithmic transformation results in Benford's Law.

A.1 Algebraic Approach

Let's first use an algebraic approach. If we want to understand the distribution of the first digits, first we have to figure out how to extract them from a normal number. Second, we will identify the range of numbers that start with any particular digit. Third, we scale this solution up to work with very large (or very small) numbers. Finally, we simplify the expression – resulting in the familiar Benford's Law formula.

A.1.1 Initial Digits

Our first challenge is to isolate the first significant digit. It's not immediately obvious how to separate those initial digits from the rest of a number. For this, it helps to write numbers in scientific notation: the same way scientists and engineers handle very small or very large numbers.

Scientific notation splits a number into two parts: a *coefficient* multiplied by 10 to some unknown *power*. For example:

- 4,500 is 4.5×10^3
- 0.01 is 1.0×10^{-2}
- –7,800,000,000 is -7.8×10^9

Let's formalize that description of scientific notation:

$$A\ Number\ (N) = Coefficient\ (C) * 10^{exponent\,(e)}$$

For Benford's Law, we care about the coefficient (C). The exponent (or the power of 10) just tells us where the decimal point goes. It doesn't affect the initial digits that Benford's Law analyzes. Note that if your data is in some base other than 10 (such as hexadecimal or octal), you would replace 10 with the appropriate number. Base invariance was discussed in Chapter 10. This notion of scientific notation explains why Benford's Law doesn't change with the change of bases: we fundamentally don't care about them. The base is isolated from our significant digits (the coefficient), so changing one doesn't influence the other.

A.1.2 Range of Values

Now that we have defined those initial digits, let's frame our question. We want to know when a certain number (n) starts with a certain digit (d). To help us understand, let's look at some examples:

- A number starts with 1 when the coefficient is between 1 and 2.
- A number starts with 2 when the coefficient is between 2 and 3.

- A number starts with 3 when the coefficient is between 3 and 4.
- etc.

We could generalize this as: a number starts with a certain digit (d) when the coefficient is between d and d+1. The range of numbers starting with that digit is just the difference between the start and end points. That is:

$$\textit{Range of numbers starting with } D = (D+1) - D$$

Remember that our numbers have been expressed in scientific notation. We need to include those powers of 10. Let's return to our definition of a number (N), but replacing those basic coefficients with our new digits:

$$\textit{Range of numbers starting with } D = (D+1) * 10^{e} - D * 10^{e}$$

This explanation is currently missing something important. It doesn't scale well. The digits between 1 and 2 all start with 1. The distance is 1 (because 2 – 1 = 1). The digits between 1,000 and 2,000 also all start with 1, but their distance is 1,000 (because 2,000 – 1,000 = 1,000)! Our formula makes sense for single-digit numbers, but doesn't make much sense for bigger numbers. What are we missing?

A.1.3 Getting Logarithmic

Our data could be very small or very large. It could be fractions of a penny or billions of dollars. It's true that the "distance" between \$1 and \$2 is 1 – but what about \$1,000 and \$2,000? What about \$1 million to \$2 million? Our current system treats that as a big difference, but really all these cases are just doubling. We need some kind of logic that recognizes the scale doesn't really matter.

The solution is the logarithm. A logarithmic scale reflects this idea of percentage growth. The distance between \$1 and \$2 will be the same as \$1,000 and \$2,000 (they are both examples of doubling). All we need to do is apply a logarithm:

$$\log\left((D+1) * 10^{e} - D * 10^{e}\right)$$

The rest of the work is just solving and simplifying this expression using the basic arithmetic properties of logarithms. First, let's get rid of subtraction:

$$log\left((D+1)*10^e - D*10^e\right) = log\left(\frac{(D+1)*10^e}{D*10^e}\right)$$

Both the top and bottom of that fraction have the power of 10 (10^e). That can be divided out to simplify the expression a bit more:

$$log\left(\frac{(D+1)*10^e}{D*10^e}\right) = log\left(\frac{D+1}{D}\right)$$

The expression is no longer based on the scale of our data. Benford's Law is expected to be true no matter how big or small our data is – so that's good news. Finally, we can do a little more division:

$$log\left(\frac{D+1}{D}\right) = log\left(\frac{D}{D}+\frac{1}{D}\right) = log\left(1+\frac{1}{D}\right)$$

This is the formula for Benford's Law presented in Chapter 2.

A.2 Visual Approach

Another way to understand Benford's Law is to *see* it. Let's start by looking at a number line for the digits 1–10. Figure A.1 is such a number line. Which numbers start with 1? Clearly, it's the numbers in the range 1–2 (not including 2 itself). The shaded area below represents that range. This is 10% of the total distance from 1 to 10.

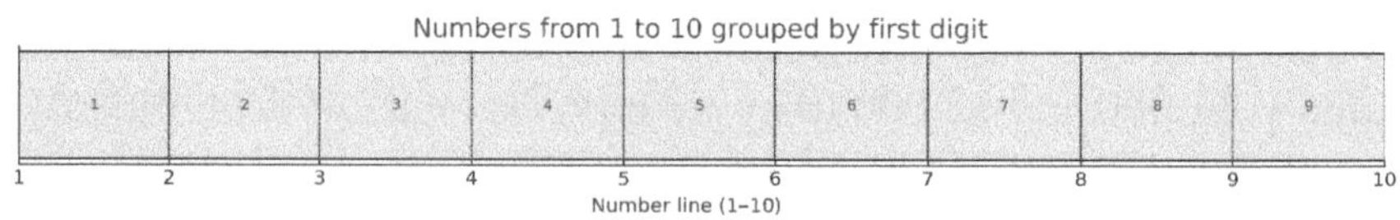

Figure A.1 Numbers from 1 to 10 grouped by first digit

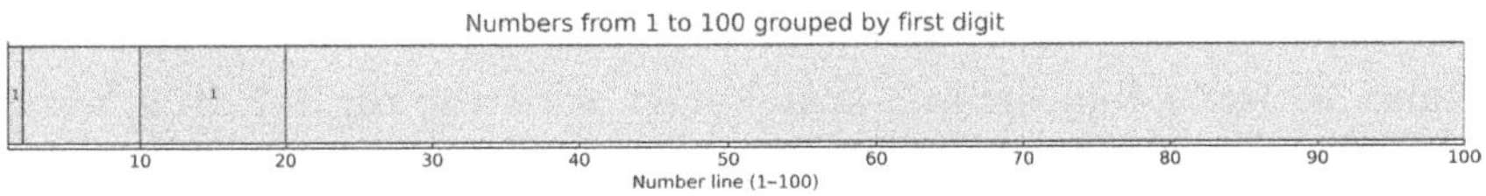

Figure A.2 Numbers from 1 to 100 grouped by first digit

What about a bigger number line, say from 1 to 100? Figure A.2 is an example. The shaded area still represents the numbers that start with 1. In this case, it's two different ranges:

- 1–2
- 10–20

Something interesting happens here. There are two "bands" where the first digit is 1. In both cases, it's 10% of the scale. For example, the band between 1 and 2 includes only numbers that start with 1. That is 10% of the single-digit numbers (1–10). Similarly, the band between 10 and 20 includes only numbers that start with 1. That is 10% of the two-digit numbers (10–100). Both are 10%.

There's a lingering visual problem. Why does the first 10% look very small, but the second 10% looks very large? Benford's Law asks "what percentage of numbers start with 1"? 10% should be the same size, no matter where on the number line it's located. How do we fix that? The solution is to use the logarithm. Figure A.3 shows the same number line on a logarithmic scale. The bands now appear to be the same size:

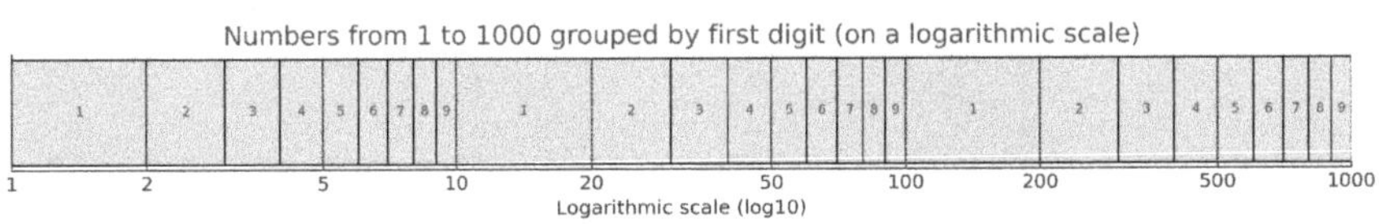

Figure A.3 Numbers from 1 to 1000 grouped by first digit (on a logarithmic scale).

Perfect! Now the pattern matches our intuition: 10% looks the same no matter where on the number line we are. This transformation also gives us the familiar pattern of Benford's Law. Below the number line is the logarithm of each value. Notice that the logarithm of 1 is 0, and the logarithm of 2 is 0.30. 30% of numbers between 1 and 10 (on a logarithmic scale) start with the digit 1. That's the number predicted by Benford's Law. You see the same number when you compare the logarithm of 100 (which is 2) to the logarithm of 200 (which is 2.3).

This is the heart of Benford's Law. When you look at data in terms of relative (or percentage growth) instead of absolute units, Benford's Law occurs naturally.

For Product Safety Concerns and Information please contact our EU
representative GPSR@taylorandfrancis.com
Taylor & Francis Verlag GmbH, Kaufingerstraße 24, 80331 München, Germany

www.ingramcontent.com/pod-product-compliance
Ingram Content Group UK Ltd.
Pitfield, Milton Keynes, MK11 3LW, UK
UKHW020207200926
475702UK00004B/649

* 9 7 8 1 0 3 2 9 1 0 3 9 0 *